CHRIS PENMAN

99 HACKS FOR WEALTH

Transform Your Wealth, Escaping Debt, Thrive – Your Guide to a Richer Life

First published by CCP Publications 2024

Copyright © 2024 by Chris Penman

©2024 Chris Penman. All rights reserved.

No part of this publication may be reproduced, distributed, or transmitted in any form or by any means, including photocopying, recording, or other electronic or mechanical methods, without the prior written permission of the publisher, except in the case of brief quotations embodied in critical reviews and certain other noncommercial uses permitted by copyright law. For permission requests, write to the publisher at CCP Publications.

The information provided within this book is for educational and informational purposes only. The author and publisher of this book and the accompanying materials have used their best efforts in preparing this book. The author and publisher make no representation or warranties with respect to the accuracy, applicability, fitness, or completeness of the contents of this book. They disclaim any warranties (expressed or implied), merchantability, or fitness for any particular purpose. The author and publisher shall in no event be held liable for any loss or other damages, including but not limited to special, incidental, consequential, or other damages. As always, the advice of a competent legal, tax, accounting, or other professional should be sought. The author and publisher do not warrant the performance, effectiveness, or applicability of any sites listed or linked to in this book. All links are for information purposes only and are not warranted for content, accuracy, or any other implied or explicit purpose.

First edition

This book was professionally typeset on Reedsy.
Find out more at reedsy.com

Contents

IMPORTANT: READ THIS FIRST	v
INTRODUCTION	x
1 UNVEILING THE MONEY MYSTERY	1
Tracking Your Treasure	1
The True Cost of Your Habits	4
Financial Leaks and How to Plug Them	7
2 DITCHING DEBT: A ROADMAP	14
Facing Your Financial Fears	14
Strategies for Swift Repayment	17
Creating a Debt-Free Future	21
3 SMART SOCIAL MEDIA SPENDING	26
Recognizing Hidden Traps	26
Curbing Online Shopping Spree	30
Using Social Media Wisely	33
4 CUTTING COSTS CREATIVELY	40
Home Efficiency Hacks	40
Transport and Travel Tweaks	44
Smarter Shopping	47
5 INCOME AUGMENTATION APPROACHES	53
Upskilling for Upliftment	53
Side Hustles for Success	57
Investing Made Intuitive	60
6 MASTERING MONEY-SAVING MINDSETS	67
The Art of Delayed Gratification	67

   Frugal Living Fundamentals   71
   Savvy Savings Tools   74

7   PROBLEM SPENDING: DIAGNOSIS AND TREATMENT   80
   Identifying Triggers   80
   Breaking Bad Habits   83
   Long-term Behavioral Changes   87

8   BUILDING FINANCIAL RESILIENCE   93
   Emergency Preparedness   93
   Navigating Financial Setbacks   98
   Strengthening Financial Health   102

9   PAVING THE PATH TO RETIREMENT   109
   Early Planning Perks   109
   Investment Strategies for the Future   112
   Lifestyle Adjustments for Later Life   116

10   CRAFTING YOUR LEGACY   122
   Estate Planning Essentials   122
   Financial Education for Your Family   125
   Charitable Considerations   130

11   CONTINUAL FINANCIAL IMPROVEMENT   137
   Staying Informed and Adaptive   137
   Using Technology to Your Advantage   141
   Reflecting and Revising Regularly   145

EMBARKING ON YOUR FINANCIAL FREEDOM JOURNEY   152

IMPORTANT: READ THIS FIRST

Hi, I'm Chris Penman, and I'm grateful you took the opportunity to get this book. You're about to embark on a transformative journey, one that will reshape your understanding of wealth and guide you towards a life of financial freedom and abundance.

For over 35 years, I've immersed myself in the world of personal finance and wealth management. Throughout my career, I've seen firsthand the confusion and misinformation surrounding financial planning and savings. It sparked my commitment to create this highly anticipated book, designed to clear the fog on money matters and lead you to the prosperous life you deserve.

After all, maybe you've tried to set a budget, only to find yourself derailed by unexpected expenses or seductive sales that seem too good to pass up. It's frustrating to see your hard-earned cash slip through your fingers, leaving you more disheartened each month.

Maybe you've even attempted to save a portion of your income, dreaming of that stress-free vacation or a comfortable retirement, only to find that at the end of the month there's hardly anything left to save. It feels like running on a treadmill, working hard but getting nowhere.

Or maybe you've even reached out for help, consulting books and financial advisors, only to be bombarded with jargon that leaves you more confused than enlightened. The entire process can feel overwhelming and isolating.

The truth is, you're not alone. It seems most are becoming a victim of the overwhelming complexity of modern-day financial systems that are designed more for the benefit of institutions than the individuals trying to navigate them.

That feeling of frustration, confusion, and isolation can be paralyzing. It's like being stuck in a thick fog, unable to see the path forward or even imagine a future where financial worries aren't constantly weighing you down.

Here's what most don't realize: the financial environment we operate in is laden with traps and pitfalls designed to prey on your aspirations and fears, making it all too easy to make mistakes that can have long-term consequences on your financial health.

And now with the possibility of economic shifts and the ever-changing landscape of retirement planning, the stakes are even higher. Understanding how to protect and grow your wealth in these times is more critical than ever.

It seems most are left in a state of perpetual anxiety, fearing that they'll never escape the cycle of paycheck to paycheck living, never experience true financial freedom, or worse, end up a financial burden to their loved ones as they age.

But it doesn't have to be this way. This book is your first step towards breaking free from these cycles and stepping into a brighter, more secure financial future.

The Perpetual Loop of Financial Frustration

Meet the Perpetual Loop of Financial Frustration – a relentless cycle that seems to ensnare those with aspirations of a richer life, filled with more disposable income and significant savings. As you step through this guide, you'll recognize the all-too-familiar stages, each one a stepping stone back to the first, shackling you to a status quo that never seems to change.

Initial Desire

The first step in this vicious cycle is Initial Desire. You want more—more comfort, more security, more luxuries. Perhaps you've eyed a new car, a better home, or dreamt of exotic vacations. This desire isn't just about material gains; it's about elevating your quality of life. But with this desire comes the stark realization of your current financial limitations.

Mismatched Actions

As the reality of your financial situation sinks in, Mismatched Actions follow. Maybe you've tried cutting back on daily coffees or opted for budget vacations instead of the luxurious getaways you dream of. Perhaps you've even tried working extra hours or taken on a side job. Yet, the numbers don't quite add up. The gap between your dreams and your bank balance seems to widen, despite your best efforts.

Temporary Relief

Then comes a phase of Temporary Relief. A bonus at work, a tax refund, or perhaps a small windfall. For a moment, the financial pressure eases. You feel a surge of optimism. "This is it," you think, "I'm finally turning a corner." You allow yourself some indulgences, celebrating these small victories. But as the fleeting euphoria fades, the fundamental issues in your financial structure remain unaddressed.

Overwhelming Complexity

Feeling momentarily richer, you might consider more complex financial advice or investment strategies. This stage, Overwhelming Complexity, sees you subscribing to financial magazines, following expert blogs, and maybe dabbling in stocks or real estate. But the complexity of financial jargon and the unpredictability of markets only add to your anxiety. The fear of making costly mistakes can paralyze your decision-making, leaving you more confused than empowered.

Illusory Stability

Finally, you enter the stage of Illusory Stability. You believe you've set everything straight. You've made a few smart moves, perhaps even grown your savings a bit. "Maybe I've cracked it this time," you hope. However, without a solid understanding of financial planning and sustainable wealth management, this stability is often short-lived. Unexpected expenses, economic downturns, or simply the rising cost of living can quickly disrupt your perceived security, sending you spiraling back to Initial Desire.

It just goes to show, you would be wise to do something different to gain 'more' and stop the pain and frustration inherent in this endless loop.

Which is why I'm glad you're reading this book because as you turn the page and start reading, you will finally get the answers and insights that you're looking for. This isn't just another guide; it's your roadmap out of the Perpetual Loop of Financial Frustration, towards a truly richer life.

INTRODUCTION

Imagine a life where your financial worries are a distant memory, where your bank balance isn't just a number, but a gateway to your dreams. Picture a future where you're not just surviving but thriving, enjoying a wealthier lifestyle with more disposable income and substantial savings. What if the path to this enriched life was not only possible but also paved with practical, easy-to-implement strategies? This is not a teaser for an elusive utopia; it's a realistic snapshot of what your life could look like, and you're holding the roadmap in your hands.

The dream of financial freedom is as diverse as it is universal. Whether it's escaping the suffocating grip of debt, mastering the art of saving, or building a legacy that spans generations, the core desire to transform our financial destiny unites us all. Yet, despite its universal appeal, wealth often feels like an exclusive club, reserved only for the few who were lucky enough to stumble upon the secret handshake. The truth? There is no secret handshake. There's only knowledge, action, and mindset—the three pillars upon which you can build your financial empire.

The world of finance can often seem wrapped in a veil of mystery, like a coded language that only a few can speak. Unveiling this mystery doesn't require a decoder ring; instead, it calls for a shift in perspective and the right guidance. That's where this journey begins—not with a complex algorithm or a risky investment strategy that promises moonshot returns, but with a fundamental understanding of what money really is: a tool. A tool that, when used wisely, can create not just wealth, but a life rich in freedom and choices.

But knowledge alone isn't enough. It's like having a map but not knowing how to read it. This is why the first step to transforming your wealth is learning the language of money. How does it work? What influences its flow? How can you harness its power? It's about seeing beyond earnings and expenses to understand the underlying currents that dictate financial success or failure.

Once you're equipped with this knowledge, the next step is action. This is where you take control, making strategic moves that alter your financial landscape. Think of it as setting sail across the financial seas. Without action, your ship—the embodiment of your financial goals—remains docked, swayed by the gentle rocking of waves but never actually going anywhere. Action might involve restructuring your debt, cutting unnecessary costs, or finding creative ways to boost your income. Each step, each decision, brings you closer to the shore of financial freedom.

However, knowledge and action will get you only so far if your mindset isn't aligned with your goals. The financial world is as much about psychology as it is about economics. Mastering money-saving mindsets isn't just about understanding the value of a pound; it's about reshaping your relationship with money. It's about moving from a mindset of scarcity, where every expense feels like a loss, to one of abundance, where every saving or investment is a step toward greater wealth. This psychological shift is critical because it turns passive knowledge and sporadic action into a consistent, proactive approach to wealth-building.

With these three core components—knowledge, action, and mindset—you're not just reading another finance book; you're drafting the blueprint of your richer life. This book isn't just about making more money. It's about changing how you think about and interact with money. It's about equipping you with the tools to not only meet your financial goals but to exceed them.

As you turn each page, you'll discover 99 hacks that cut through the noise and hone in on actionable, effective strategies that can be implemented right away. These hacks aren't just theoretical; they're practical, tested, and tailored to fit into your daily life without overwhelming you. From tackling debt head-on and leveraging social media for economic gain to creative cost-cutting and income augmentation, each chapter builds on the last, creating a comprehensive guide that addresses every aspect of your financial health.

The journey to wealth is not a sprint; it's a marathon. It's not about quick fixes or shortcuts but about setting a sustainable pace that you can maintain in the long run. This book is your training plan, designed to strengthen your financial muscles, boost your fiscal stamina, and prepare you for the ups and downs of the economic race.

As you embark on this journey, remember: the goal is not just to transform your wealth but to transform your life. It's about creating a financial foundation that supports your deepest desires and highest aspirations. Whether you're looking to pave the path to retirement or craft a legacy that impacts future generations, the principles contained within these pages will guide you every step of the way.

So, take a deep breath and prepare to turn your financial dreams into reality. The road to a richer life starts here.

1

UNVEILING THE MONEY MYSTERY

"A fool and his money are soon parted." - **Thomas Tusser**

Tracking Your Treasure

HACK 1- Budgeting Basics

Let's cut to the chase: knowing where your money goes each month isn't just good practice—it's essential. Think of it as the bedrock upon which your financial fortress is built. Without a budget, you're navigating a thick fog without a compass. But with one? You're the captain of your ship, steering clear of icebergs.

Start simple. A budget is just a plan for how to spend your money based on how much you expect to bring in. First, jot down your total monthly income after taxes—this is your starting line. Next, list out your essential expenses: rent or mortgage, utilities, groceries, and transport costs. These are your non-negotiables, the must-haves for basic living.

Now, let's talk about the discretionary spend—this is where it gets fun (and tricky). These are expenses like dining out, entertainment, and that cheeky weekend getaway. It's crucial to allocate funds here too, because let's be honest, life isn't just about covering the essentials.

The magic happens when you subtract your total expenses from your income. The number left over? That's your potential savings. If it's in the negative, don't panic! This is your financial roadmap, and now you know what needs tweaking.

Remember, budgeting isn't about restricting—it's about making informed choices. It empowers you to channel your funds where they'll make the biggest impact on your wealth and happiness.

HACK 2- Using Financial Tracking Apps

Gone are the days of scribbling budgets on napkins or trying to do mental math with your bank statements. Enter the era of financial tracking apps—your new best friends in the quest for financial clarity.

Apps like Mint, YNAB (You Need A Budget), or Pocketbook sync with your bank accounts and categorize your spending automatically. They can help you set up budgets, monitor expenses, and even provide you with alerts if you're about to overspend in a category.

Why use an app? Because what gets measured gets managed. With these tools, you can see a real-time snapshot of your financial health. Over time, you'll start to notice patterns in your spending that you might have missed otherwise. Maybe you're spending a lot more on dining out than you realized, or perhaps your utility bills have crept up unnoticed.

Another pro tip: use these apps to set financial goals. Want to save for a deposit on a house or fund a dream vacation? Set it as a goal, and these apps can help you figure out how much you need to save each month to make it happen.

HACK 3- Analyzing Monthly Expenses

Now that you're equipped with a budget and a shiny new app, it's time to dive deeper into your spending habits. This is where you transform from being reactive about your finances to being proactive.

Each month, take some time to go through your expenses. Look beyond the numbers; what do they tell you about your financial behavior? Are there subscriptions you forgot about but are still paying for? Are you spending a significant portion of your income on things that don't really add value to your life?

This analysis isn't just about cutting costs—it's about refining your spending to align more closely with your values and goals. Perhaps you find joy in cooking at home rather than dining out. Maybe you realize that a gym membership isn't worth it because you prefer running outdoors.

Also, keep an eye on the irregular expenses that don't occur monthly but can cause significant financial strain if not planned for—things like car maintenance, insurance premiums, or annual memberships. These can be budget busters if they catch you off guard.

By regularly analyzing your expenses, you'll start to see where you can make adjustments that don't just save money, but also enhance your financial wellbeing. It's about making your money work for you in the most efficient way possible.

Through these steps—establishing a budget, leveraging technology, and conducting monthly expense analyses—you're not just tracking your treasure; you're increasing it. Each pound saved or spent wisely is a step closer to a richer life, paving the way for more disposable income and robust savings for the future.

The True Cost of Your Habits

Let's face it, every pound you spend on that frothy cappuccino or dine-out can add up over time. You might not think much of these little indulgences, but they could be the silent budget-killers lurking in your daily routine. Understanding the true cost of your habits is not just about cutting back mindlessly; it's about making smarter choices that enrich your life financially and personally.

HACK 4- Daily Coffees vs. Homemade

Imagine starting every morning with a quick visit to your favorite coffee shop. The smell of freshly ground beans, the cozy ambiance, a cup of coffee made just the way you like it—sounds perfect, right? Now, let's talk numbers. Say your coffee costs £3.50, a seemingly small amount. Multiply this by the number of working days in a year, say 260, and you're looking at £910 annually on coffee alone.

Switching to homemade coffee can dramatically slash this expenditure. Investing in a good coffee maker and buying quality beans might seem like a steep upfront cost, but it pays off. For instance, even if you spend £100 on a coffee machine and £10 a month on beans, your yearly expense drops to £220. That's a saving of £690 every year, just from brewing your own coffee! This doesn't just save money; it saves time you'd spend queuing, and you gain the skill of making your perfect cup at home.

HACK 5- Cost of Eating Out

Dining out is another area where many casually overspend. It's convenient, social, and gives you a break from cooking. However, the costs can be eye-wateringly high compared to eating at home. A meal that costs £25 per person at a restaurant could often be made at home for a quarter of the price—or even less.

Let's crunch some numbers. Dining out three times a week at £25 a meal racks up to £3,900 annually per person. Now, if you were to redirect even one of those meals to a home-cooked dinner costing around £6, you could save over £1,000 per year. Not only is cooking at home cheaper, but it also allows you to control ingredients, portions, and thus, your health. You don't need to cut out restaurant visits entirely but think of them as a treat rather than a routine.

HACK 6- Impulse Purchases Impact

Lastly, let's tackle the bane of many budgets: impulse purchases. These are often spurred by emotions—excitement, stress, the thrill of a bargain—not necessity. Whether it's a new outfit, the latest gadget, or even a snack at the checkout, impulse buying can make a serious dent in your savings.

To put it into perspective, if you spend £30 weekly on items you didn't plan to buy, that totals £1,560 a year. That's a significant chunk of change that could go towards your savings or debt repayment. Curbing impulse purchases starts with awareness. Before you buy, ask yourself: Do I need this? Can I afford it? Is there a cheaper alternative? By pausing to consider these questions, you can avoid unnecessary spends and keep your budget intact.

Moreover, setting a 'cooling-off' period for larger purchases helps. Wait a few days before buying to determine if it's something you really need or just a fleeting desire. Often, the urge to buy diminishes over time.

Incorporating these practices into your daily routine doesn't just save money; it also cultivates financial discipline that benefits all areas of your life. Each pound saved is a step closer to your financial goals, be it debt repayment, a significant purchase, or a comfortable retirement. Treat personal finance like a skill, improving with practice and patience, and watch as your relationship with money transforms from casual spending to strategic investment in your future.

Financial Leaks and How to Plug Them

Let's dive right into the sneaky streams that slowly drain your wallet without you even realizing it. Think of your financial life as a ship sailing towards the island of prosperity. Now, what would happen if your ship had leaks? It'd struggle to reach the destination, right? Well, your financial leaks are pretty much the same, and it's crucial to address them before you can truly sail smoothly towards a richer life.

HACK 7- Subscription Audits

First up, let's talk about subscriptions. In today's digital age, it's easy to get hooked on multiple subscriptions — from streaming services to fitness apps, and even those meal kits. While each of these might seem like small amounts, they cumulatively bleed more cash than you might realize.

Start with a simple audit. Look through your bank statements and identify every single subscription. You'll likely find at least one or two you forgot you had. Yes, even that app you downloaded for a free trial and never canceled qualifies. The next step? Determine what you actually use. This isn't just about finding what you enjoy but scrutinizing what brings real value to your life.

For each subscription, ask yourself:- How often do I use this service?- Is it essential for my work or wellbeing?- Can I find a cheaper or free alternative that works just as well?

If a subscription doesn't make the cut, cancel it. And here's a pro tip: consider annual subscriptions for the ones you decide to keep. Many companies offer a hefty discount for paying yearly instead of monthly.

HACK 8- Reducing Utility Usage

Moving on, let's tackle the utilities. Energy bills can be a significant monthly expense, especially if you're not mindful about usage. Small changes can lead to substantial savings, and honestly, you won't even feel the pinch.

Start with the basics — lighting. Switching to LED bulbs can save you a chunk of change as they consume less energy and have a longer lifespan than traditional bulbs. Next, look at your heating and cooling expenses. Smart thermostats can be game changers as they adjust the temperature based on your schedule and preferences, ensuring you're not heating an empty house or overcooling an unused room.

Water bills can also be reduced with some smart tweaks. Fixing leaks and installing water-efficient fixtures like low-flow showerheads and dual-flush toilets can significantly reduce your water usage. These might seem like small tweaks, but over a year, they add up to noticeable savings.

And remember, it's not just about being frugal; it's about being smart. Appliances left on standby mode still consume energy. So, switch off appliances at the plug when not in use. It's a simple habit that saves energy and money — a win-win!

HACK 9- Tackling High-Interest Debts First

Lastly, let's address probably the most significant leak: high-interest debt. Credit card debt, payday loans, store cards — these are not just debts; they're anchors that drag you down by accumulating interest at an alarming rate.

The strategy here is simple yet powerful — the avalanche method. Focus on paying off the debt with the highest interest rate first while maintaining minimum payments on others. Once the highest debt is paid off, move to the next highest, and so on. This method saves you money on interest payments and speeds up the debt elimination process.

It's crucial to stop adding new charges to these accounts. Lock away those cards if you must, and switch to using cash or a debit card. Seeing real money leave your wallet can have a psychological impact and can curb spending.

Consider transferring balances to a lower interest rate card if possible. Many credit cards offer introductory periods with low or no interest, which can give you a breather and help you reduce the balance more quickly. Just be wary of transfer fees, and make sure you have a plan to pay off the balance before the promotional period ends.

Eliminating these debts frees up a significant portion of your income — money that can be redirected towards savings, investments, or even splurging on yourself occasionally without guilt.

By plugging these financial leaks — auditing subscriptions, reducing utility usage, and tackling high-interest debts — you're not just saving money; you're taking active steps towards a more stable and prosperous financial future. Each small step is a building block in crafting a lifestyle where you control your money, not the other way around. Keep at it, and soon enough, you'll find yourself not just surviving, but thriving.

RECAP AND ACTION ITEMS ON THE

9 UNVEILING THE MONEY MYSTERY HACKS

Congratulations on making it through this illuminating exploration of your financial landscape! By now, you've equipped yourself with some powerful insights to navigate the often-murky waters of personal finance. Let's briefly recap what you've uncovered and outline some steps you can take to solidify these new habits.

Firstly, by tracking your treasure through budgeting basics, utilizing financial apps, and analyzing your monthly expenses, you've laid the groundwork for a solid financial structure. This isn't just about knowing where your money goes – it's about actively directing it to work for you.

Next, we delved into the true cost of your habits. It's eye-opening, isn't it? Seeing how daily coffees, eating out, and impulse purchases can add up over time shows just how much potential there is for saving. Remember, every pound saved is a pound that could be earning you interest elsewhere.

Lastly, you've identified and started plugging those financial leaks. Whether it's canceling unused subscriptions, cutting back on utility usage, or prioritizing high-interest debts, each step you take is a move towards greater financial freedom.

Now, for the action steps. Here's what you can do to keep the momentum going:

Implement a Budgeting Tool:

Choose one of the financial tracking apps we discussed and make it a daily habit to check in. This will help you stay on top of your expenses and keep your financial goals in sight.

Create a 'Luxury Fund':

Instead of buying that coffee or lunch out, put the equivalent amount of money into a savings pot. Use this for something truly meaningful, like a much-needed holiday or an investment in a passion project.

Regular Subscription and Utility Reviews:

Mark a date every three months in your calendar for a subscription audit and a utility usage review. This regular check-in ensures you don't slip back into old habits.

Debt Snowball Method:

If you haven't already, start with paying off your smallest debt first while making minimum payments on others. Once the smallest debt is paid off, move to the next smallest. This method can be highly motivating and financially liberating.

By taking these actions, you're not just dreaming of a richer life; you're actively building it. Remember, wealth isn't just about having money—it's about having choices. The more you implement these strategies, the more choices you open up for yourself and your future. So, go ahead, take control, and watch as your new, wealthier lifestyle begins to take shape.

2

DITCHING DEBT: A ROADMAP

"The borrower is slave to the lender." – **Proverbs 22:7**

Facing Your Financial Fears

Embarking on a journey to financial freedom can often feel like preparing to scale a towering mountain. It's daunting, filled with unknowns, and yes, it can be downright scary. But, just as every seasoned climber knows, the summit is reached step by deliberate step. The first of these steps? Facing your financial fears head-on.

HACK 10- Listing All Debts

The foundation of overcoming any fear is understanding exactly what you're up against. When it comes to financial fears, it's essential to start by laying all your cards on the table. This means creating a comprehensive list of every single debt you owe — from the smallest to the largest. Why? Because you can't tackle what you don't know.

Grab a piece of paper, open a spreadsheet, or use one of the many apps designed for budgeting. Record each debt, including details such as the creditor's name, the total amount owed, the interest rate, and the monthly payment required. This might include credit card debts, student loans, a mortgage, personal loans, and even money owed to friends or family.

This exercise does more than just quantify your debts. It visualizes your financial obligations, which can be an eye-opening experience. Seeing everything written down can shift your mindset from feeling overwhelmed to being empowered. Knowledge, after all, is power.

HACK 11- Prioritizing Debt Repayment

With your debts laid bare, the next step is to decide the order in which you'll tackle them. There are a couple of popular methods here: the snowball method and the avalanche method. While you'll get a deeper dive into these strategies in the next section, here's a quick overview to help you start prioritizing.

The snowball method involves paying off your debts from smallest to largest, regardless of interest rate. This method can offer quick wins, boosting your motivation and sense of accomplishment. On the other hand, the avalanche method focuses on paying off debts with the highest interest rates first, which can save you money on interest payments over time.

Consider what feels more sustainable for you. Do you thrive on immediate gratification and could benefit from the psychological boost of clearing smaller debts quickly? Or are you more motivated by overall efficiency and saving on interest costs?

Once you've chosen your strategy, rearrange your debt list accordingly. This prioritized list becomes your roadmap. Stick to it, adjust as necessary, and remember, each payment is a step closer to debt freedom.

HACK 12- Seeking Professional Advice

Tackling debt isn't always a solo journey. In fact, seeking professional financial advice can be a game-changer, especially if your debts are complex or causing you significant stress.

A financial advisor or a debt counselor can offer tailored advice based on your specific circumstances. They can help you understand all your options, from restructuring your debts to potentially consolidating them into a single, more manageable payment. They might also assist in negotiating with creditors on your behalf to secure lower interest rates or more favorable repayment terms.

Remember, there's no shame in seeking help. Just as you

wouldn't hesitate to consult a doctor for a physical ailment, consulting a financial professional for debt management is a smart move. It's about equipping yourself with expert insights and tools to navigate your way out of debt more efficiently.

Moreover, many communities offer free or low-cost counseling services, so look into what's available in your area. You might be surprised at the resources you can access without straining your budget further.

By confronting your financial fears through these three practical steps — listing all debts, prioritizing their repayment, and seeking professional advice — you're not just planning to get out of debt; you're counseling to win back your financial freedom. Each action you take builds momentum, turning fear into empowerment, and transforming what once seemed like an insurmountable challenge into a series of achievable goals. Remember, every great journey begins with the courage to take that first step. So, take a deep breath, and let's step forward together.

Strategies for Swift Repayment

When you're knee-deep in debt, the journey ahead can seem like an uphill trek without a clear path. However, with a strategic approach, it's entirely possible to clear the fog and find your way to financial freedom quicker than you might think. Let's break down some effective strategies that can help speed up your debt repayment.

HACK 13- Snowball vs. Avalanche Methods

Debt repayment isn't just about paying back what you owe; it's about finding a method that you can stick with without losing motivation. Two popular strategies that have helped countless individuals regain control are the Snowball and Avalanche methods.

The Snowball method is all about momentum. Picture a small snowball rolling down a snowy slope, gathering more snow and size as it goes. This is how you tackle your debts: start with the smallest debt first, regardless of interest rate. Pay it off as quickly as possible while making minimum payments on your other debts. Once the smallest debt is paid off, you roll the amount you were paying on that debt into the next smallest debt, and so forth. This method can be incredibly motivating because you see results quickly; debts disappear one by one, which can give you the psychological boost to keep going.

On the other hand, the Avalanche method takes a more mathematical approach and focuses on saving you money on interest over time. Here, you list your debts from the highest interest rate to the lowest. You focus all your extra repayment capacity on the debt with the highest interest rate, while paying the minimum on others. Once the most expensive debt is cleared, you move on to the next highest interest rate. This method can be slower in terms of seeing individual debts disappear, but it's efficient in reducing the amount of interest paid over time.

Both methods have their merits, and your choice might depend on what motivates you more: quick wins or overall efficiency. Some find that starting with the Snowball method helps them build the discipline and joy in paying off debt, eventually switching to the Avalanche method to finish off their remaining debts efficiently.

HACK 14- Consolidating Debts

If you're juggling multiple debts with varying interest rates, consolidation might be your ticket to a simpler and potentially cheaper repayment plan. Debt consolidation involves taking out a new loan to pay off multiple debts, leaving you with just one monthly payment rather than several. The goal here is to secure this new loan at a lower interest rate than the average of your existing debts, which can reduce the amount you pay in the long run.

There are various ways to consolidate debt, including personal loans, balance transfer credit cards, and home equity loans. Each has its pros and cons, and the right choice depends on your specific financial situation as well as the nature of your debts. A balance transfer credit card, for example, often offers an introductory 0% APR for a set period, which can be a powerful tool if you can pay off a significant portion of the debt during this time. However, be wary of transfer fees and the standard interest rate once the introductory period ends.

It's essential to crunch the numbers and possibly speak to a financial advisor to ensure that consolidation makes sense for you. Remember, consolidation isn't about giving you license to rack up more debt; it's about reducing your debt burden more efficiently.

HACK 15- Negotiating Lower Interest Rates

Sometimes, the simplest way to speed up your debt repayment is to reduce the cost of your debt. Reach out to your creditors to negotiate lower interest rates on your credit cards or loans. It might sound daunting, but many creditors are willing to work with you, especially if you've been a good customer and have made your payments on time.

Start by reviewing your current interest rates and understanding what might be competitively available from other institutions. Armed with this information, call your creditor, explain your situation, and ask if they can offer you a lower rate. Be polite but persistent. Remember, it's in their interest to keep you as a paying customer. Even a small reduction in your interest rate can save you significant amounts over the life of your debt and can free up more money to go towards the principal each month.

Tackling debt repayment needn't be a dreary slog. By choosing the right strategy, consolidating wisely, and negotiating better terms, you can accelerate your journey out of debt and closer to financial freedom. The key is to stay proactive, stay motivated, and keep your eyes on the prize—a life where your finances are no longer a source of stress, but a foundation for future prosperity.

Creating a Debt-Free Future

HACK 16- Automating Savings

In the grand scheme of things, automating your savings is like setting up a silent, hard-working buddy who's always looking out for your financial health, even when you're not. Think about it: every time you earn, you save. It's not just any form of saving; it's the kind that happens without you having to lift a finger after the initial setup. This nifty trick is what can transform your financial trajectory from precarious to prosperous.

Let's dive into the 'how'. First, you need to set up a direct debit from your current account to your savings account, scheduled right after your payday. Why after payday? Because you won't miss what you don't see. By making your savings automatic, you effectively make your lifestyle fit your remaining budget, rather than saving what might be left at the end of the month—which, let's be honest, often turns out to be less than we hoped.

But where should this money go? Into a high-interest savings account, where it can grow. The beauty of compound interest means that over time, your money doesn't just increase; it multiplies. This is the closest thing to magic in the financial world. Over the years, even modest regular deposits can grow into a substantial nest egg, thanks to the interest compounding upon itself.

Now, you might be wondering, "How much should I save?" While the exact figure can vary depending on your circumstances, a good rule of thumb is to aim for at least 20% of your net income. If that sounds steep, start lower and increase the amount gradually. The key is consistency and making sure it's realistic; there's no point in setting up an automatic transfer that you'll need to dip into regularly, as that defeats the purpose.

HACK 17- Building an Emergency Fund

Next up, let's forge your financial safety net: the emergency fund. This isn't just any savings account. It's your financial buffer against unexpected expenses that could otherwise plunge you back into debt. Think boiler breakdowns, job loss, or any large, unforeseen bills. Having an emergency fund means these situations don't have to derail your financial stability.

How much should be in this fund? Ideally, enough to cover three to six months' worth of living expenses. It sounds daunting, but you don't have to fund this overnight. Start small, even if it's just £20 or £50 a month. Every little contribution builds resilience into your budget.

Store this fund in an accessible, yet separate, savings account. It needs to be immediately available when you need it, but not so accessible that you're tempted to dip into it for everyday spending. Online banks often offer good rates and easy access, making them a solid option for your emergency stash.

Remember, the purpose of this fund is to cover essentials, not luxuries. It's about survival, not comfort. That distinction is crucial. Once you start building this fund, you might find a sense of relief knowing that you're prepared for the unexpected. It's like an insurance policy funded by, and for, yourself.

HACK 18- Regular Financial Reviews

Last, but definitely not least, is the habit of conducting regular financial reviews. This might sound tedious, but it's about as exciting as discovering money you didn't know you had. Regular reviews allow you to adjust your plans based on changing circumstances and ensure you're always in control of your financial path.

Set a recurring appointment with yourself every three to six months. During this review, assess your income, expenses, savings progress, and whether your financial goals align with your current lifestyle or long-term aspirations. Are you saving enough? Are there new expenses to consider? Could you be investing?

This is also the perfect time to celebrate your successes. Have you reached a savings milestone? Reduced your expenses? Recognizing your achievements provides motivation and reinforces positive financial behaviors.

Moreover, use this time to tweak your budget. Maybe you've paid off a debt and can redirect that money into savings. Perhaps you've gotten a pay rise and can increase your savings rate. Life isn't static, and neither should your budget be.

In conclusion, automating savings, building an emergency fund, and conducting regular financial reviews aren't just steps; they are pillars on which you can build a robust, resilient financial future. By implementing these strategies, you're not just escaping debt; you're paving a path to a wealthier, more secure life where financial surprises are mere inconveniences, not crises. This is how you equip yourself not just to survive, but to thrive.

RECAP AND ACTION ITEMS ON THE

9 DITCHING DEBT HACKS

You've now ventured through the essential steps to ditching debt and paving the way to a wealthier, more secure financial future. By confronting your financial fears, adopting savvy repayment strategies, and setting the stage for a debt-free life, you're on the right track to transforming your wealth.

Start by reflecting on your debt list and prioritizing which debts to pay off first. Whether you choose the snowball method to gain momentum with small victories or the avalanche method to tackle high-interest debts, the key is consistency and commitment. Remember, each payment is a step towards your financial liberation.

Consider consolidating your debts if you're juggling multiple payments. This could not only simplify your monthly finances but potentially lower the interest rates you're battling against. Speaking of rates, don't hesitate to negotiate for lower interest rates. You'd be surprised how often creditors are willing to offer a reduction to facilitate repayment.

Moving forward, automating your savings isn't just about setting money aside; it's about building a buffer that keeps you from falling back into debt. Make it a point to review and adjust your automated savings as your financial situation improves or changes. Meanwhile, an emergency fund is your financial safety net. Start small if you must, but start. Even a modest emergency fund can prevent you from spiraling back into debt due to unforeseen expenses.

Lastly, keep a regular check on your financial health with frequent reviews. This isn't just about tracking where you are but also about adjusting your strategies to fit new goals or rectify past oversights.

Your journey to a richer life isn't about drastic changes, but about making smarter choices consistently. Equip yourself with these tools, and you'll not only escape debt but thrive in newfound financial freedom. Let each step you take be purposeful and driven towards that richer life you aspire to. Remember, the road to wealth is paved with proactive financial decisions!

3

SMART SOCIAL MEDIA SPENDING

"Too many people spend money they haven't earned, to buy things they don't want, to impress people they don't like." - **Will Rogers**

Recognizing Hidden Traps

Imagine you're scrolling through your favorite social media platform, and suddenly, you find yourself purchasing something you didn't need, or feeling a little less confident about your financial choices compared to others. Sounds familiar? You're not alone. Social media, while being a powerful tool for connection and information, can also be a playground for spending triggers and emotional comparison. Let's dissect these hidden traps one by one, helping you navigate through them and keep your wallet happier.

HACK 19- Advertisement Influence

Firstly, let's talk about how ads on social networks can make you spend money without you hardly noticing. These platforms have become incredibly adept at tailoring advertisements based on your browsing habits, likes, and even the content you and your friends discuss. Before you know it, you're seeing ads for that gadget you mentioned in a comment or that pair of shoes you lingered on during your last online shopping spree.

To combat this, start by being more mindful of your online behavior. Notice how after searching for a specific item, advertisements for similar items pop up across different platforms? That's no coincidence. It's targeted advertising at play. Companies spend millions to ensure that their products catch your eye in just such a way. To outsmart this trap, limit the information you share on social platforms. Adjust your privacy settings to reduce the amount of data social media platforms can collect about you. This might mean turning off certain permissions on your app settings, being cautious about what you post, or even reviewing the privacy terms to better understand how your data is being used.

Moreover, give yourself a 'cooling-off' period before making a purchase you see advertised on social media. If after 24 to 48 hours the product still seems as essential as it did when you first saw it, then it might be worth considering. Often, giving yourself time to think can help reduce impulse buys fueled by clever advertising.

HACK 20- Social Comparison

Now, onto the more psychological aspect of social media — the comparison game. It's easy to fall into the trap of comparing your behind-the-scenes with everyone else's highlight reel. When you see friends and influencers flaunting their latest purchases, luxurious holidays, or just their seemingly perfect lives, it can stir up feelings of inadequacy and spur financial decisions that you might not ordinarily make.

Remember, what you're seeing is often a curated version of reality. Most people aren't posting about their struggles, their debt, or the sacrifices they made to afford that new luxury car. To keep this trap at bay, actively remind yourself that these posts are just snippets of a larger reality. Engage with social media mindfully and intentionally; consume content that makes you feel good about your journey and your achievements, no matter the scale.

Furthermore, consider curating your feed. Follow accounts that promote budgeting tips, financial advice, or personal growth. This can transform your social media from a source of spending pressure into a motivational tool that encourages smarter financial habits.

HACK 21- In-app Purchases

The third trap sneaks in through in-app purchases. These are especially prevalent in mobile games and applications, where buying something can feel as simple and inconsequential as clicking a button. From extra features, subscriptions, to premium content, in-app purchases can quickly accumulate and take a toll on your finances without you even realizing it.

To dodge this effectively, scrutinize every app before downloading. Check if it offers in-app purchases and critically assess if you really need these extras. Could you do without them? Also, many apps offer a one-time payment for an ad-free experience, which might be more economical in the long run compared to frequent in-app purchases.

Setting a budget specifically for in-app purchases is another practical approach. Most smartphones allow you to set spending limits for such purchases, or you could set up a monthly budget for small luxuries, including these digital buys. Once you hit your limit, no more spending until the next cycle.

By understanding these traps and adjusting your interaction with social media, you can protect yourself from unnecessary expenditure and mental clutter. Recognizing these hidden influencers in your digital life is the first step towards smarter financial health and a richer, more contented life.

Curbing Online Shopping Spree

In an era where a single click can deplete your bank account, mastering the art of resisting online shopping sprees is crucial. Let's dive into practical strategies to help you navigate the tempting waters of digital consumerism without capsizing your financial boat.

HACK 22- Unsubscribing from Marketing Emails

The first line of defense against excessive spending is often the simplest yet most overlooked: managing your inbox. Marketing emails are not just friendly updates; they are finely honed tools designed to pull you back into spending. Each "exclusive offer", "limited time deal", or "just for you discount" is crafted to create a sense of urgency that can be hard to resist.

Start by scrutinizing your email subscriptions. How many of these do you truly read, and how many lead to impulsive purchases? The reality is, if you didn't wake up thinking about buying a specific item, you probably don't need it, no matter how enticing the sale might seem.

The process of unsubscribing might feel tedious, but modern email providers often offer tools to simplify this process. Look for options to unsubscribe from promotional emails en masse. Alternatively, services like Unroll.me can help you manage your subscriptions effectively by consolidating them into a single daily digest or making it easier to unsubscribe from unwanted emails in bulk.

Remember, every unopened email is a small victory against impulse spending. By reducing the noise, you clear a path to make more mindful decisions about when and where to spend your money.

HACK 23- Installing Ad Blockers

The next tool in your arsenal is the ad blocker. As you navigate the web, ad blockers work quietly in the background, shielding you from the relentless barrage of online advertisements. These ads are not just annoying distractions; they are triggers designed to make you spend money on things you don't need.

Installing an ad blocker on your browser can significantly reduce these triggers. It's like putting on a virtual blindfold to avoid the visual temptations scattered across the internet. Whether it's banner ads, pop-ups, or video ads, blocking them lessens the chances of getting lured into an unplanned spending spree.

There are plenty of free and paid ad blockers available, such as Adblock Plus, uBlock Origin, or AdGuard. They are generally easy to install and can be customized according to your browsing preferences. Some even offer the ability to whitelist sites whose content you trust and want to support. This way, you're not just protecting your wallet but also curating a cleaner, faster, and more enjoyable online experience.

HACK 24- Setting Spending Alerts

The final piece of the puzzle in curbing your online shopping spree is to set up spending alerts. Most banks and credit card companies offer this feature, which can be a game-changer in how you manage your finances. These alerts notify you when you've made a purchase, or when your spending reaches a certain threshold that you've predefined.

Imagine getting an instant message every time you make a transaction. It forces you to acknowledge the spending, which can be quite sobering if you're trying to cut back. Additionally, setting a monthly spending limit for leisure and non-essential items helps keep your financial goals in check. When you approach the limit, you'll receive an alert, giving you a chance to pause and reflect on whether you truly need to make any more purchases.

Setting up these alerts is typically straightforward. Log into your online banking portal or app, and look for the notifications or alerts section. From there, you can customize what triggers an alert, be it the amount spent or the type of transaction. This real-time feedback on your spending habits can be incredibly powerful in helping you stick to your budget.

By integrating these strategies—unsubscribing from marketing emails, installing ad blockers, and setting spending alerts—you equip yourself with a robust set of tools designed to fend off impulsive purchases. Each method works to interrupt the cycle of spontaneous buying, granting you the time and clarity needed to make financial decisions that align with your long-term wealth goals. With these defenses in place, you can navigate the digital shopping realms more safely, ensuring that your online activities contribute positively to your financial well-being rather than undermining it.

Using Social Media Wisely

In an era where our digital interactions can be as frequent and as meaningful as our real-world interactions, social media isn't just a leisure activity—it's a tool. And like any tool, its effectiveness depends on how we use it. Here, we explore three strategic ways you can harness social media to not only enhance your wealth but also empower your lifestyle.

HACK 25- Educational Content Over Entertainment

Let's face it, the allure of cat videos and meme pages is strong. But when was the last time you finished a social media session feeling genuinely enriched or better equipped to tackle your financial goals? Probably not recently. Here's a hack: pivot your focus towards consuming content that can educate and inspire you to grow your wealth.

Start by following financial gurus, economic institutions, and business news outlets. These can be treasure troves of valuable information, providing daily insights into market trends, investment tips, and financial advice. But don't stop there. Engage actively with the content. Comment with questions, share with peers to start discussions, and even write your own reflective posts on what you've learned. This active engagement helps reinforce your new knowledge—transforming passive scrolling into an educational session.

Moreover, many platforms like Instagram and YouTube now host live webinars and workshops led by experts. These sessions often end with a Q&A segment where you can ask specific questions that relate to your personal financial situation. Participate in these spaces. It's like attending a finance class, only without the hefty tuition fees.

HACK 26- Promoting Personal Businesses

If you run a personal business or are considering it, social media is a goldmine for marketing—without the gold expense. Platforms like Facebook, Instagram, and Pinterest offer powerful tools to reach new audiences. The key here is not just to promote, but to connect. Share your journey, the highs and lows. People resonate with authenticity and are more likely to support a business with a face and story they feel connected to.

Consider showcasing customer testimonials, behind-the-scenes videos, or even educational content related to your product or service. For instance, if you're selling skincare products, posts about skin care routines or the science behind your ingredients can be informative and indirectly promote your products.

Furthermore, utilize the advertising tools these platforms offer. With targeted ads, you can ensure that your business is being seen by those who are most likely to be interested in what you have to offer. This minimizes expenditure and maximizes impact. Dive into analytics to understand which posts are doing well and why, then refine your strategy accordingly. Remember, every post is an opportunity to both add value and draw attention to your business.

HACK 27- Networking Opportunities

Finally, let's talk networking. Social media is a networking event that never ends. It's filled with professionals from across the globe who could be potential mentors, partners, clients, or customers. LinkedIn, known for its professional network, is an obvious place to start. Regularly updating your profile and engaging with other people's content can increase your visibility and credibility in your field.

However, don't underestimate the power of other social networks. Twitter, for instance, is a fantastic platform for real-time conversations. Follow industry leaders and participate in relevant hashtag discussions. These can be gateways to new insights and connections. Join Facebook groups related to your business or financial interests. These groups are often filled with like-minded individuals and can be a great source of support, advice, and new opportunities.

When engaging on these platforms, always bring value to the conversation. Share your expertise, ask insightful questions, and offer help where you can. Networking is a two-way street—the more you put in, the more you'll get out. Keep your interactions professional and respectful, and remember that every comment or post builds your online persona and reputation.

In summary, transforming your social media usage into a wealth-building tool requires a shift in how you view and interact with these platforms. Choose education over entertainment, utilize social media for business promotion, and dive into the networking possibilities. By doing so, you not only enrich your understanding and control of personal finances but also open doors to opportunities that could lead to significant financial growth. Remember, on social media, you're in the driver's seat. Navigate wisely.

RECAP AND ACTION ITEMS ON THE

9 SMART SOCIAL MEDIA SPENDING HACKS

Congratulations on progressing through the vital insights of Smart Social Media Spending. By now, you've equipped yourself with the knowledge to recognize the hidden traps of the digital world, curb those impulsive online shopping sprees, and harness the power of social media for productive purposes. Let's solidify this learning with actionable steps that you can start implementing today to steer your financial future towards more wealth and less waste.

Audit Your Social Media Influence

Take a moment to reflect on how advertisement influences, social comparison, and in-app purchases have impacted your spending. Begin by reviewing your last month's bank statements and identify charges that were influenced by social media. This will help you see the real impact and motivate you to make changes.

Clean Up Your Inbox and Browser

Start by unsubscribing from marketing emails. Services like Unroll.me can help you see all your subscriptions in one place, making this task easier. Next, install ad blockers on your browsers to reduce the temptation from incessant ads. This simple action can significantly decrease spontaneous buys.

Set Spending Alerts

Most financial apps now offer the option to alert you when you're nearing a set spending limit. Take advantage of this feature. Set a reasonable budget for different categories of spending, especially for discretionary items, which are often influenced by social media.

Shift Your Focus on Social Media

Allocate your social media time more towards educational content that can enrich your knowledge and skills rather than mere entertainment. Follow influencers and thought leaders who inspire you to grow financially and personally.

Leverage Social Media for Growth

If you have a personal business or a side hustle, use social media as a free marketing tool. Also, don't underestimate the power of networking; connect with individuals who can offer career advice, investment tips, or partnership opportunities.

By following these steps, you'll not only reduce unnecessary expenditure but also enhance your income potential. Remember, every swipe, click, or like is a decision. Make those decisions count towards building a wealthier and more fulfilling life. Start today, because the best time to take control of your financial destiny is now.

4

CUTTING COSTS CREATIVELY

"Beware of little expenses; a small leak will sink a great ship." - Benjamin Franklin

Home Efficiency Hacks

In the quest to bolster your bank account and elevate your lifestyle, mastering the art of home efficiency is akin to discovering a secret passage to untapped wealth. It's not just about cutting costs; it's about smart living where every penny saved is a penny earned. Let's dive into the nitty-gritty of how you can transform your home into a bastion of efficiency and cost-effectiveness.

HACK 28- Energy-Saving Appliances

The first port of call in your journey toward an efficient home is the very machines that make modern life a breeze. Yes, we're talking about your appliances. Outdated appliances are not just aesthetic eyesores; they are voracious energy hogs that stealthily inflate your electricity bills.

The shift to energy-saving appliances might sound like an investment—and it is—but it's one that pays dividends in the long run. Look for products boasting the Energy Star label, a hallmark of efficiency. These appliances use anywhere from 10% to 50% less energy each year than their non-efficient counterparts. Consider this: replacing an old refrigerator alone can save you up to £150 annually on energy bills.

When shopping for these efficient marvels, focus on the most used appliances in your home. The refrigerator, washing machine, dishwasher, and boiler are typically the big players. For instance, opting for a washing machine with a high-efficiency rating and a 'quick wash' option can significantly reduce the energy and water used per cycle.

HACK 29- DIY Repairs

Next up, let's tackle the DIY repairs. Before you groan at the thought of donning your DIY hat, consider this: learning to fix minor issues in your home can save you a hefty sum that would otherwise go to professional repair services. With a plethora of tutorials available online, becoming a competent DIY repairer has never been easier.

Start with the basics: dripping taps, running toilets, and simple electrical issues like changing out light fixtures or replacing a faulty switch. These are typically straightforward fixes that you can master with a few online videos and some basic tools. Not only do these repairs reduce your maintenance costs, but fixing leaks promptly also prevents wasteful water usage, ticking another box in your efficiency checklist.

For more ambitious projects, such as installing insulation, consider whether you're up for the challenge or if it might be more cost-effective—and safer—to hire a professional. Remember, the goal is to save money without compromising on safety or quality.

HACK 30- Water Usage Reductions

Water might seem cheap, but wastage can lead to an ocean of unnecessary expense over time. Reducing water usage is a dual win—it's good for the planet and your pocket. Here are a few hacks to get you started:

Install Water-Saving Fixtures:

Low-flow showerheads and taps can dramatically reduce water use without you even noticing a difference in flow. These fixtures are relatively inexpensive, easy to install, and can save thousands of liters of water annually.

Fix Leaks Promptly:

A leaking tap can waste over 5,500 liters of water a year. Regularly check your pipes and faucets for leaks and address them immediately. This is where your newfound DIY skills will come in handy.

Be Smart with Water Heating:

If you're using an immersion heater or a boiler, ensure it's insulated. This keeps water hotter for longer, reducing energy use. Also, setting the thermostat on your water heater to 60°C ensures you're not overheating your water (and your energy bill).

Use Water Wisely:

Simple changes in habits can lead to significant savings. For instance, running your dishwasher only when it's full or using a water butt to collect rainwater for gardening can contribute to reducing your water footprint.

Implementing these hacks won't just cut down your bills overnight. It's about setting up a system and cultivating habits that ensure sustained savings. Think of your home as a small ecosystem where efficiency and mindfulness pave the path to a wealthier lifestyle. By focusing on these areas, you're not just saving for today; you're investing in a richer tomorrow. So, take these steps, one at a time, and watch as your home transforms into a haven of cost-effectiveness and environmental responsibility.

Transport and Travel Tweaks

HACK 31- Carpooling

Let's kick things off with carpooling, a tried and tested way to cut down your travel expenses dramatically. Think about it: if you're commuting to work alone, you're not just burning fuel, but also burning a hole in your wallet. Carpooling is the smart solution to this; it's like splitting the bill at a restaurant, but for your daily travel.

The beauty of carpooling lies in its simplicity and the immediate benefit it offers. By sharing rides with colleagues or friends, you can halve or even quarter your monthly fuel costs. But the benefits don't stop at just saving money. You'll be reducing wear and tear on your car, and less driving means lower maintenance and repair costs over time. Plus, fewer cars on the road mean less traffic congestion and a smaller carbon footprint.

To get started, check if your workplace offers a carpool scheme. If not, take the initiative and start one. Use apps like BlaBlaCar or websites like Liftshare to find people in your area who travel the same route. Remember, communication is key to a successful carpool, so make sure you discuss schedules, pick-up points, and contributions to fuel costs upfront.

HACK 32- Public Transport

Switching gears, let's talk about public transport. If carpooling isn't an option, or you want to leave the car at home altogether, buses, trains, and trams can be your wallet's best friends. In many cases, traveling by public transport can be significantly cheaper than driving, especially when you factor in all the associated costs of car ownership.

To maximize savings, invest in a season ticket – most transport services offer significant discounts for monthly or annual passes. If you're in London, for example, an Oyster card can provide substantial savings over single-journey tickets. Also, many public transport systems offer further discounts during off-peak hours, so consider adjusting your travel times if your schedule allows.

But here's a pro tip: combine public transport with a bit of walking or cycling. Not only will you save money, but you'll also get your daily dose of exercise. Plus, in congested cities, sometimes walking or biking can be faster than any other form of transport.

HACK 33- Cheaper Travel Booking Tips

Lastly, let's unpack some secrets to booking travel without breaking the bank. Whether it's a local weekend getaway or an international adventure, knowing how to book can save you a fortune.

Start with flexibility. If you can be flexible about when you travel, you're already ahead. Flying midweek can often save you pounds as flights are usually cheaper on Tuesdays, Wednesdays, and Thursdays. Also, flying out early in the morning or late at night can sometimes offer savings; these less desirable times can be your golden ticket to cheaper fares.

Comparison sites are your friend here. Use platforms like Skyscanner or Google Flights to compare prices across a whole month. This way, you can spot the cheapest days to fly at a glance. Remember, though, while these sites are useful, it's always wise to double-check the airline's own website, as some deals might be exclusive to their site.

And don't forget about alternative airports. Flying into a smaller, less busy airport can sometimes lead to better fares. For instance, if you're visiting Paris, consider flying into Beauvais Airport instead of Charles de Gaulle. Yes, it might be a bit further out, but the savings on your flight could make the extra travel worthwhile.

Booking accommodation can also be optimized for savings. Consider rental platforms like Airbnb or budget hotels that offer kitchen facilities. This way, you can save on eating out by cooking some meals yourself. Also, look for last-minute deals; hotels often reduce prices at the last minute to fill rooms.

So, there you have it. Implementing these tweaks to how you manage transport and travel can not only save you money but also enhance your travel experience by making it less stressful and more enjoyable. Whether it's everyday commuting or occasional travel, every penny saved is a penny that can be used to enrich your life in other meaningful ways. Remember, it's not about cutting corners; it's about spending smarter and living richer.

Smarter Shopping

HACK 34- Bulk Buying

Let's kick things off with a powerful, yet often overlooked, tactic to manage your finances better: bulk buying. The principle behind bulk buying is simple – purchasing larger quantities of goods can significantly reduce the cost per unit. This practice isn't just for big families or for those with ample storage space; even solo shoppers can harness the power of bulk buying with a bit of savvy planning.

Start by identifying products that you use regularly and that have a long shelf life. Items like rice, pasta, toilet paper, and canned goods are ideal candidates. These are products that won't spoil quickly and can be stored easily. Next, keep an eye on offers at wholesale clubs or bulk sections in supermarkets. Membership fees for wholesale clubs can seem off-putting at first, but the savings on bulk items can offset this cost quite quickly.

It's also worth considering splitting bulk purchases with a friend or neighbor if storage space or upfront cost is a concern. This way, you both benefit from lower prices without the worry of waste or finding space for a year's supply of toilet paper!

Another angle to explore is the use of digital platforms that offer bulk buying options with direct delivery. This not only saves money but also time and effort in transporting heavy or bulky items. By integrating bulk buying into your shopping routine, you can make noticeable reductions in your monthly expenditures.

HACK 35- Couponing

Moving on to couponing – it's not just a relic of past shopping strategies but a goldmine for saving money if used correctly. With the digital age, couponing has transformed, and you no longer need to spend Sunday mornings clipping paper coupons. Digital coupons can be found with a simple search online or through apps dedicated to helping you save money.

To start, identify the retailers or brands you frequently shop with and subscribe to their newsletters. Often, companies send exclusive coupons and deals through these channels. Additionally, websites and apps like Honey or VoucherCodes can automatically apply discount codes at checkout, ensuring you never miss out on a saving opportunity.

However, the key to effective couponing is organization. Keep track of the coupons you have and their expiry dates. A simple spreadsheet or a dedicated folder on your email can help manage this. Also, be mindful not to buy items you don't need just because you have a coupon. The goal of couponing is to save money on purchases you would make anyway, not to encourage unnecessary spending.

HACK 36- Seasonal Shopping Strategies

Lastly, let's dive into seasonal shopping strategies. Prices on various goods fluctuate throughout the year based on demand, seasonality, and overstock. By planning your purchases according to these cycles, you can save a substantial amount.

For starters, understand the best times to buy certain items. For instance, electronics are typically cheaper during new model releases as retailers make room for new stock, and January sales are ideal for purchasing holiday decorations for the next year at a fraction of the cost. Clothing also follows a seasonal pattern; buying out of season can save you a bundle. Swimwear in autumn and coats in spring are usually on sale as stores clear out last season's stock.

Additionally, keep an eye on major sales events such as Black Friday, Cyber Monday, and Boxing Day. These events can offer significant savings on a variety of items, from appliances to furniture to tech gadgets. Preparation is key here – plan what you need in advance and set a budget to avoid impulse buys.

Moreover, consider the timing of your grocery shopping. Visiting the supermarket in the evening can often yield reduced prices on perishable goods that need to be sold by the end of the day. Many stores discount items like bread, meat, and fruits as closing time approaches.

By incorporating these smarter shopping practices into your routine, you're not just saving pennies; you're paving the way towards a more financially liberated lifestyle. Remember, the goal isn't merely to spend less, but to spend smart and save more. Consider these strategies as tools in your financial toolkit, enabling you to enhance your savings and live a richer life without compromising on your needs or quality of life.

RECAP AND ACTION ITEMS ON THE 9 CUTTING COSTS CREATIVELY HACKS

Congratulations on powering through some game-changing ways to streamline your expenses and boost your financial health! You've now equipped yourself with savvy strategies across home efficiency, transport and travel, and smarter shopping. Let's cement these insights with actionable steps to ensure you're not just absorbing information but actively transforming your wealth.

Home Efficiency Hacks:

Start by evaluating your current appliances and note which ones could be upgraded to energy-efficient models. This might seem like a pricey step initially, but the long-term savings on energy bills will be worth it. Next weekend, why not tackle one DIY repair? Whether it's fixing a leaky tap or insulating your windows, each small step will reduce your utility bills. Lastly, monitor your water usage by installing low-flow showerheads and taps. Remember, every drop counts when it comes to saving money.

Transport and Travel Tweaks:

This week, explore carpooling options for your daily commute by connecting with colleagues or using a carpooling app. Not only will this cut down your travel costs, but it's also better for the environment. For longer journeys, become familiar with the public transport routes and schedules—it could be more convenient than you think. Also, make it a habit to compare travel prices online and book in advance to snatch those early-bird rates.

Smarter Shopping:

Bulk buying is your new best friend. Identify non-perishable goods you frequently use and purchase them in bulk for substantial savings. Combine this with a routine of clipping coupons or using digital coupon apps to slash prices even further. Lastly, mark your calendar for seasonal sales which offer the best deals, ensuring you're buying at the lowest prices.

By integrating these practices into your daily life, you're not just cutting costs; you're paving the way for a richer, more financially secure future. Remember, the key to wealth isn't just about how much you earn but also how much you save and optimize your spending. Let these tweaks bring you closer to the financial freedom you aspire to achieve. Keep pushing forward, and watch your savings grow!

5

INCOME AUGMENTATION APPROACHES

"An investment in knowledge pays the best interest." - Benjamin Franklin

Upskilling for Upliftment

In today's fast-paced world, staying relevant in your career isn't just a suggestion; it's a necessity. If you're looking to boost your income and secure a more financially stable future, upskilling is your ladder to climb higher. Not only can it lead to promotions and better job opportunities, but it also puts you in a position to negotiate higher salaries or pivot into entirely new industries. Let's dive into how you can enhance your skill set and make yourself irresistibly valuable in the marketplace.

HACK 37- Online Courses

The digital revolution has democratized learning, bringing the classroom to your living room, café, or anywhere you choose. Online courses are a goldmine for anyone looking to expand their horizons without breaking the bank or rearranging their life around school schedules. Platforms like Coursera, Udemy, and LinkedIn Learning offer courses in everything from blockchain technology to digital marketing, most of which are designed to fit into a busy lifestyle.

Investing in an online course is about more than just acquiring knowledge; it's about applying this new knowledge in ways that directly enhance your earning potential. For instance, mastering Excel through an online course isn't just about learning the functions but about analyzing data more efficiently, leading to better business decisions. Similarly, a course in web development can enable you to build websites, a skill highly sought after in the freelance market.

The key here is to select courses that offer practical skills, align with your career goals, and come with some form of certification that you can flaunt on your CV and LinkedIn profile. Remember, the goal isn't just to learn; it's to turn that learning into earning.

HACK 38- Certification Programs

While online courses are great for broad learning, certification programs are the power tools for nailing specific skills and showing undeniable proof of your expertise. These are particularly useful in fields where certification is not just beneficial but required for career advancement. Fields like project management, IT, and healthcare offer various certifications that are recognized globally and can significantly boost your professional credibility.

Think about certifications like the Project Management Professional (PMP)® or Certified Information Systems Security Professional (CISSP)®. These aren't just acronyms to add after your name; they're badges of honor that scream competence and dedication to your profession. They tell potential employers that you're committed to your field and capable of handling high-responsibility roles.

Moreover, many companies are willing to pay a premium for certified professionals. In fact, it's not uncommon for certain certifications to lead to an increase in salary, as they set you apart from the crowd. The investment in a certification program often pays for itself several times over, making it a wise financial decision for anyone looking to elevate their career.

HACK 39- Networking Events

While upskilling technically is crucial, never underestimate the power of who you know. Networking events provide a platform not just to meet new people but to exchange ideas, pitch your skills, and even find mentors. They can be particularly useful when you're trying to break into a new field or looking to climb up the ladder in your current one.

Attending industry conferences, seminars, and even informal meet-ups can open doors that you didn't even know existed. For instance, that casual conversation you strike up over coffee could lead to a job offer, a business partnership, or at the very least, a tip about an upcoming opportunity in your field.

To get the most out of networking events, go in with a strategy. Have a clear idea of what you want to achieve – be it learning about new industry trends or meeting potential employers. Prepare an elevator pitch that succinctly showcases your skills and experiences. And most importantly, follow up. A quick LinkedIn message or email thanking someone for their time can go a long way in cementing a new relationship.

By combining new skills through online courses and certifications with strategic networking, you're not just preparing for the future; you're actively building it. This proactive approach to professional development not only makes you more attractive to potential employers but also equips you with the tools to launch your own ventures should you decide to tread the path of entrepreneurship.

Each step you take in upskilling opens a new door, adding not just to your knowledge base but also to your bank account. In the modern economy, your skills are your currency. Make sure you're rich in knowledge and watch as opportunities to increase your wealth follow.

Side Hustles for Success

HACK 40- Freelancing

In an era where your financial destiny can feel like it's held by the whims of employers, there's something revolutionary about freelancing. It's about taking back control, leveraging your skills, and tapping into a global market that's hungry for what you can offer. Whether you're a wizard with words, a software savant, or a graphic design guru, there's likely a freelancing opportunity out there for you.

Starting out, platforms like Upwork, Freelancer, and Fiverr can be your launching pad. These sites allow you to create a profile showcasing your skills and bid on projects that match your expertise. The key here is to start small and scale up. Your initial goal isn't necessarily to earn big but to build a robust portfolio and gather positive reviews.

Pricing your services initially can be more art than science. A good strategy is to peek at what others in your niche are charging. Don't undervalue your service; price fairly based on your skills and the complexity of the tasks. As you grow in confidence and portfolio, gradually increase your rates. Remember, in freelancing, your time is your most valuable asset. Efficient time management can multiply your effective hourly rate without needing to work more hours.

Networking shouldn't be overlooked either. Connect with other freelancers and industry professionals on LinkedIn or within your local community. Often, jobs come from referrals and having a robust network can mean the difference between feast and famine.

HACK 41- E-commerce

Then there's the digital storefront world of e-commerce—a realm where your entrepreneurial spirit can truly soar. Launching an online store might sound daunting, but platforms like Shopify, WooCommerce, and Etsy have made it more accessible than ever. These platforms handle a lot of the heavy lifting, allowing you to focus on what you sell rather than how to code a website.

The first step is choosing a niche. What are you passionate about? What do you understand better than most? Whether it's handmade crafts, vintage clothing, or the latest tech gadgets, finding a niche can help you carve out a dedicated customer base. Remember, the most successful e-commerce businesses solve real problems or fulfill genuine desires.

Inventory management is another crucial aspect. You can opt for dropshipping, where you sell products that are shipped directly from a supplier to your customer, eliminating the need to keep items in stock. This method reduces overhead but can come with longer shipping times and less control over product quality.

Marketing your store is where the magic happens. Utilize social media platforms to reach potential customers. Platforms like Instagram, Pinterest, or Facebook can be particularly effective, depending on where your target market hangs out. Consider using targeted ads to boost your reach initially, and don't forget the power of content marketing—blogs, videos, and posts that engage and inform can drive traffic to your store.

HACK 42- Rental Income

Perhaps the most traditional route in our list, yet still highly effective, is generating rental income. This could be from property you own, but let's not overlook the potential of rentable items such as tools, equipment, or even parking spaces. Platforms like Airbnb have also opened the door to renting out spare rooms or entire properties for short stays.

If you're considering property rental, the first step is understanding your market. What kind of properties are in demand in your area? Who are your potential tenants? This understanding can dictate everything from the location you choose to buy or rent out, to the price you set.

For those not ready to purchase property, consider subletting a room in your house or renting your home while you're away on holiday. If you go down this route, ensure you have the necessary permissions from landlords or mortgage providers and that you're abiding by local regulations.

Maintenance is a crucial part of being a landlord. Keeping properties well-maintained not only keeps tenants happy but can also prevent costly repairs down the line. Consider setting aside a percentage of rental income for maintenance and emergencies.

Lastly, understand the legal side of things. Tenancy agreements, property law, and your rights and responsibilities as a landlord are crucial areas to understand to protect yourself and your assets.

Each of these side hustles requires effort, persistence, and a willingness to learn and adapt. Whether you choose freelancing, e-commerce, or delving into the rental market, the key to success lies in your commitment to see it through, coupled with a constant eye for opportunities to optimize and expand your new income stream. Embrace the journey, and watch as your financial landscape transforms.

Investing Made Intuitive

HACK 43- Stock Markets for Beginners

Diving into the stock market can seem like navigating a vast ocean in a rowboat. But guess what? With the right toolkit, even you can steer like a seasoned captain. Let's demystify the process and break down the essentials, making it as easy as pie to get started in the stock market.

First things first, you need to understand what stocks are: shares in the ownership of a company. When you buy a stock, you're buying a piece of that company, making you a shareholder. If the company does well, so do you; if it doesn't, your stock value may decrease.

Now, where do you start? Set up a brokerage account. This is much simpler than it sounds. Online platforms like Hargreaves Lansdown or Interactive Investor can guide you through the process. They offer user-friendly interfaces and resources to help beginners. Plus, setting up an account can be as quick as signing up for a new social media profile.

Once your account is set up, it's time to think about what stocks to buy. Start with what you know. Are you a tech enthusiast? Consider tech companies. Love fashion? Look at retail sectors. Investing in industries you're familiar with gives you a leg up, as you're more likely to know when something significant happens.

Before you make any purchases, though, it's crucial to do your research. Look at the company's health: are they making money? Are they growing? What does the competition look like? Also, consider broader market conditions. Is the overall market strong? Are there external factors that could influence stock prices?

When you're ready to buy, start small. Remember, the stock market is not a sprint; it's a marathon. You can begin by investing a small amount and gradually increase as you become more comfortable and your financial situation improves.

Finally, keep a long-term perspective. Stock prices will fluctuate, sometimes dramatically, but over the long term, the stock market has trended upwards. Patience pays off.

HACK 44- Real Estate Basics

Real estate investment is another excellent way to build wealth over time. It's tangible, generally stable, and something you can use creatively to generate income, whether through rental income or capital appreciation.

The simplest way to start is by buying property to rent out. The key here is location, location, location. Properties in high-demand areas, near transport links, schools, and amenities, are typically easier to rent out and can command higher rents.

However, getting into real bleeding estate requires more up-front capital compared to stocks. You'll need money for the down payment, and possibly for fixing up the property. But don't let this deter you. If direct ownership seems too hefty at first, consider real estate investment trusts (REITs). These are companies that own or finance income-producing real estate and are a way to invest in real estate without having to actually buy property. You can buy shares of a REIT just like stocks, often with a smaller amount of capital.

If you decide to go the direct route and purchase property, make sure to do your due diligence. Understand all the costs involved, not just the purchase price. Consider property taxes, maintenance, insurance, and potential periods when the property might be vacant.

Also, think about your target tenants. Are they students, families, or professionals? This will influence the type of property you buy and how you market it.

Like stocks, real estate should be viewed as a long-term investment. Property values can fluctuate, but they generally appreciate over time. Moreover, rental properties can provide a steady income stream, helping to cushion any downturns in property values.

HACK 45- Peer-to-Peer Lending

Peer-to-peer lending is a relatively new kid on the block but has quickly become a popular investment option. It allows you to lend money directly to individuals or businesses through online platforms, bypassing traditional financial institutions.

The allure here is the potential for higher returns compared to traditional savings or investment routes. Platforms like Funding Circle or RateSetter facilitate these transactions. You can choose whom to lend to, how much, and at what interest rate. The risk and return vary depending on who you lend to and the terms of the loan.

It's important to diversify your loans. Don't put all your eggs in one basket. By spreading your investment across different borrowers and loan types, you can mitigate the risk of default.

Another consideration is liquidity. Your money will be tied up for the duration of the loan, which could range from a few months to several years. Some platforms offer a secondary market where you can sell your loan to other investors, but this is not guaranteed.

Finally, understand the platform's fees and the default process. What happens if a borrower fails to repay? What measures does the platform have to recover your money?

Peer-to-peer lending can be a rewarding investment, offering attractive returns if managed wisely. Like all investments, however, it requires due diligence and a clear understanding of the risks involved.

By exploring these three accessible investment avenues, you can start to diversify your portfolio and increase your financial resilience. Each has its unique features and risks, but with informed decisions and strategic planning, you can navigate these waters successfully, paving the way for a wealthier, more secure future.

RECAP AND ACTION ITEMS ON THE

9 INCOME AUGMENTATION APPROACHES HACKS

By now, you've armed yourself with a powerhouse of strategies to elevate your income and jumpstart a wealthier lifestyle. It's about turning knowledge into action and seeing tangible results in your bank account and beyond.

Let's begin with upskilling. The digital age has unlocked unlimited potential through online courses, certification programs, and networking events. Identify skills that are in demand and align with your passions or career goals. Whether it's learning to code, digital marketing, or project management, enhancing your capabilities can lead to promotions, raises, or entirely new career opportunities. Commit to enrolling in at least one course or attending a networking event this month. Remember, the connections you make could be just as valuable as the skills you acquire.

Next, explore side hustles that resonate with your lifestyle and interests. Freelancing offers flexibility and the opportunity to capitalize on your existing skills. Platforms like Upwork or Freelancer can get you started. E-commerce, on the other hand, lets you tap into the vast online market—consider starting small with items you are knowledgeable about. Lastly, if you have an extra room or a second property, think about generating passive income through rental. Evaluate what you can offer and take the first step by listing a service or product this week.

Lastly, investing is not just for the wealthy; it's for anyone who wants to build a sustainable financial future. Start with the basics of the stock market or real estate investments. Peer-to-peer lending platforms can also offer returns and help diversify your investment portfolio. Open a demo account or attend a workshop to demystify these concepts before committing your hard-earned money.

The journey to a richer life begins with these steps. Choose one action from each category and set a deadline to complete them. Wealth isn't built overnight, but through consistent, informed, and strategic actions. You've got this! Let's make your financial growth unstoppable.

6

MASTERING MONEY-SAVING MINDSETS

"Do not save what is left after spending, but spend what is left after saving." - Warren Buffett

The Art of Delayed Gratification

In a world where instant gratification is just a click away, mastering the art of delayed gratification might just be your golden ticket to wealth transformation. It's about playing the long game, focusing on the bigger picture rather than the immediate rewards. By adopting this mindset, you set yourself up not just for short-term gains but for long-term financial freedom. Let's delve into the essentials of delayed gratification: setting savings goals, employing visualization techniques, and establishing effective reward systems.

HACK 46- Setting Savings Goals

First things first, to truly master delayed gratification, you need to set tangible, realistic savings goals. It's like setting the destination in your sat nav before you start driving. Without a clear destination, how do you choose the best route?

Start by defining what you're saving for. Is it a deposit for a house, a new car, an emergency fund, or perhaps a retirement nest egg? Once you know what you're aiming for, break it down into manageable milestones. For instance, if you want to save £20,000 for a house deposit in the next five years, set a goal to save £4,000 a year, or about £333 a month.

This breakdown makes the goal seem less daunting and more achievable, which psychologically reinforces your saving behavior. It's also essential to be specific about your goals. Instead of saying "I want to save more," determine exactly how much more. This specificity not only keeps you focused but also makes it easier to track your progress.

Remember, flexibility is key. Life throws curveballs, and your financial situation can change. Regularly reviewing and adjusting your goals ensures they remain relevant and attainable, keeping you motivated throughout your saving journey.

HACK 47- Visualization Techniques

Visualization isn't just for athletes or performers; it's a powerful tool for financial success too. By visualizing your financial goals, you can boost your motivation and stay focused on the long-term rewards rather than succumbing to short-term temptations.

Start by creating a vivid mental image of what achieving your goal will look like. Imagine the moment you make the final payment for your new home, or picturing yourself living comfortably in retirement. Feel the emotions associated with achieving these goals, whether it's relief, joy, or security. This emotional connection makes your goal more real and tangible, fueling your drive to save.

You can enhance this technique by creating physical representations of your goals. Set up a vision board in a place where you see it daily. Populate it with images representing your goals, like pictures of your dream house, travel destinations, or even a content retirement lifestyle. These visual cues serve as constant reminders of what you're working towards, making it easier to bypass immediate gratifications for future benefits.

HACK 48- Reward Systems

Finally, let's talk about reward systems, an often overlooked but crucial aspect of mastering delayed gratification. While it's great to focus on long-term goals, occasionally rewarding yourself for short-term achievements keeps your journey enjoyable and sustainable.

Establish mini-rewards for when you hit smaller milestones. For example, if your goal is to save £4,000 a year, you might treat yourself to a modest dinner out or a new book each time you save the first £1,000. These rewards should be proportionate to the milestone achieved and should not counteract your overall saving goals. The key is to choose rewards that give you satisfaction without derailing your progress.

It's also beneficial to align your rewards with your personal values and interests. This personalization makes the reward more meaningful and satisfying, increasing the likelihood of sticking to your savings plan. For instance, if you value experiences over material goods, your reward could be a day out exploring a new town instead of buying a physical item.

Incorporating a reward system not only makes the process of saving more enjoyable but also reinforces the positive behavior of saving. Each time you reward yourself, you're acknowledging your hard work and discipline, which strengthens your savings habit.

In conclusion, delayed gratification is not about denying yourself enjoyment but about prioritizing your financial future. By setting clear savings goals, visualizing your success, and rewarding yourself along the way, you cultivate a mindset that values long-term benefits over short-term pleasures. This approach doesn't just apply to saving money; it's a powerful strategy for achieving any significant goal in life. Embrace it, and watch as it transforms not just your finances, but your entire approach to life's challenges and rewards.

Frugal Living Fundamentals

HACK 49- Minimalist Lifestyle

Embracing a minimalist lifestyle isn't just about decluttering your house or choosing only to own a certain number of shirts. It's about prioritizing what truly matters to you and shedding the excess that doesn't add value to your life. This approach can significantly reduce your financial burdens and align your spending with your most deeply held values.

When you adopt a minimalist lifestyle, you make conscious decisions about what enters and stays in your life, be it possessions, activities, or relationships. This naturally limits frivolous spending because you're less likely to buy things that don't serve a defined purpose. The beauty of minimalism is found in its simplicity and the peace and clarity that come from it. Imagine your home as a space with only things that serve a purpose or bring you joy—this is the ultimate goal of minimalism.

Start small; declutter a single drawer, then a room, and eventually, your entire living space. Each item you choose to keep should have a clear reason for being in your life. Does it serve a function? Does it bring you joy? If the answer is no, then perhaps it's time to let it go. This practice will not only free up physical space but also help you make more mindful choices about future purchases, ensuring each item you buy is something needed or truly desired.

HACK 50- Avoiding Luxury Brands

It's easy to fall into the trap of equating luxury brands with higher quality, but this is not always the case. Many luxury items are priced high due to their perceived prestige rather than their functional value. By steering clear of luxury brands, you can save a substantial amount of money without compromising on quality.

Start by re-evaluating what quality means to you. Often, mid-range brands offer the same functionality and durability at a fraction of the price. It's about finding the best value for your money. Conduct thorough research before any purchase. Read reviews, compare products, and check out consumer reports. Sometimes, the less flashy brands provide goods that are just as good, if not better, than their luxury counterparts.

Moreover, consider the cost-per-use of items rather than just the upfront cost. An expensive watch might seem like a splurge, but if you wear it every day for ten years, the cost-per-use might justify the expense. The key here is to ensure that you're making purchases based on long-term value rather than instant gratification or status symbols.

HACK 51- Repair Over Replace

In today's throwaway culture, there's a prevailing idea that once something breaks, it's easier and sometimes cheaper to replace it rather than fix it. However, adopting a repair-over-replace mindset not only saves money but also instills a sense of responsibility and resourcefulness.

Start by learning some basic repair skills in areas relevant to your life. Whether it's mending clothes, fixing a leaky tap, or troubleshooting common electronic issues, these skills can be invaluable. There are countless resources online, from tutorials to forums where enthusiasts share advice and guidance. Investing time in learning these skills can pay off significantly by prolonging the life of your possessions.

Furthermore, consider the environmental impact of constantly replacing items. Repairing and maintaining what you already own reduces waste and consumption, contributing to a healthier planet. It's also deeply satisfying to fix something with your own hands—it can increase your appreciation for your possessions and reduce the likelihood of impulse buys.

By integrating these three fundamentals into your daily life, you can transform your financial landscape. A minimalist lifestyle helps you focus on what's essential, avoiding luxury brands keeps your spending in check, and opting to repair over replace fosters a deeper understanding of value and sustainability. Each of these practices not only supports your financial goals but also contributes to a more thoughtful and intentional way of living.

Savvy Savings Tools

When it comes to amplifying your financial health, the right tools can make all the difference. Just as a skilled craftsman wouldn't tackle a job without the right wrench or hammer, a smart saver needs the best tools in their financial toolkit. Let's dive into three powerful instruments: high-interest savings accounts, ISAs, and automatic transfer setups. These tools are not just mechanisms for storing your money; they are levers to enhance your financial future.

HACK 52- High-Interest Savings Accounts

Imagine you're a farmer, and every pound you save is a seed. Planting these seeds in fertile soil will yield more crop. In the financial world, a high-interest savings account is that fertile soil. It's an essential for anyone looking to grow their savings beyond the measly returns offered by standard bank accounts.

Traditional savings accounts might offer comfort and convenience, but the interest rates can be laughably low. Switching to a high-interest savings account can be a game changer. These accounts offer higher interest rates, meaning your money grows faster without any additional risk or effort on your part.

Finding the best account can feel like navigating a labyrinth. Interest rates, fees, access to funds, and bonuses vary widely.

Start by comparing the Annual Equivalent Rate (AER), which shows you potential earnings over a year. Look for accounts with the highest AER but ensure they align with your access needs. Some accounts offer splendid rates but restrict access to your funds or require a high minimum balance.

Don't overlook online-only banks. Without the overheads of traditional banks, they often offer more competitive rates. However, always ensure the bank is covered by the Financial Services Compensation Scheme (FSCS), guaranteeing your money up to £85,000.

HACK 53- ISAs (Individual Savings Accounts)

Next in your financial toolkit should be the Individual Savings Account, or ISA. This isn't just any savings account—it's a tax superpower for UK savers. You can stash away money and not pay a penny on the interest, dividends, or capital gains you earn. It's like having a financial cloak of invisibility from HMRC on the growth of your savings.

There are several types of ISAs—Cash ISAs, Stocks and Shares ISAs, Innovative Finance ISAs, and Lifetime ISAs. Each serves different needs and risk appetites. Cash ISAs are similar to regular savings accounts but with a tax-free wrapper. They are perfect if you're looking for a no-risk place to grow your savings tax-free.

For those willing to stomach some risk for potentially higher returns, Stocks and Shares ISAs invest your money in the stock market. The returns can be higher compared to cash ISAs, but remember, your capital is at risk, and you could get back less than you invest.

The Lifetime ISA is particularly compelling if you're under 40. You can contribute up to £4,000 each year until you're 50, and the government adds a 25% bonus to your savings. That's up to £1,000 free every year. You can use this towards your first home or save it until you're 60 for retirement.

HACK 54- Automatic Transfer Setups

Automation is the silent guardian of your financial growth. It's about making your good intentions fail-proof. By setting up automatic transfers, you ensure that a portion of your income is saved or invested before you have the chance to spend it. Think of it as putting your savings on autopilot.

Start by setting up a monthly automatic transfer from your checking account to your savings account right after payday. It doesn't have to be a vast amount. Even small, consistent contributions can snowball over time thanks to compound interest. The key is consistency. As you adjust to your budget over time, you can increase the transfer amount.

Automatic transfers aren't just for savings; they can also be your ally in investing. Setting up a direct debit into an ISA or a mutual fund spreads your investments over time, a strategy known as 'pound-cost averaging'. This approach can help reduce the risk of entering the market at the wrong time.

Implementing these automatic systems does more than just grow your wealth; they cultivate financial discipline by default. You learn to live on what's left after saving, rather than saving what is left after spending.

By leveraging these savvy tools—high-interest savings accounts, ISAs, and automatic transfer setups—you equip yourself not just to save money, but to transform those savings into future wealth. Each tool serves a unique purpose and fits differently into individual financial strategies, but together, they form a robust foundation for securing and growing your financial future. Remember, in the world of personal finance, being equipped with the right tools can be just as important as having the right knowledge.

RECAP AND ACTION ITEMS ON THE

9 MASTERING MONEY HACKS

You've just armed yourself with powerful insights into mastering money-saving mindsets that can transform your financial reality. Let's distill this into actionable steps to ensure you don't just walk away with knowledge but with a plan to make that knowledge work for you.

First, embrace the art of delayed gratification. Set clear, achievable savings goals and keep them in sight—literally. Craft a visual reminder of what you're working towards, be it a photo of your dream home or a chart on your fridge tracking your savings progress. This isn't just about waiting; it's about making strategic choices now to enjoy substantial rewards later. Begin today by defining one short-term and one long-term financial goal. Remember, the sweetness of gratification grows with time.

Next, streamline your lifestyle with the fundamentals of frugal living. Assess your current possessions and spending habits. Do you really need everything you own, or could you live happily with less? Challenge yourself this month to avoid purchasing luxury brands and see how it affects your bank balance. Also, the next time an appliance breaks down or a piece of clothing tears, look into repairing before you replace. This practice not only saves money but also cultivates a mindset of valuing what you have.

Finally, leverage savvy savings tools. If you don't already have one, open a high-interest savings account this week. Look into Individual Savings Accounts (ISAs) to maximize tax-free saving opportunities. Set up automatic transfers from your checking account to your savings account, ensuring you pay yourself first. Even a small, regular transfer can mount up significantly over time, turning your spare change into a cornerstone of your future wealth.

By embedding these practices into your daily life, you're not just saving money; you're investing in a future where financial stress is reduced and possibilities are expanded. Start small if you must, but do start. Every journey to a richer, more secure life begins with the decision to take control of your financial destiny.

7

PROBLEM SPENDING: DIAGNOSIS AND TREATMENT

"Never spend your money before you have it." - Thomas Jefferson

Identifying Triggers

When you find yourself caught in the whirlwind of spontaneous purchases or drowning in debt from recurrent splurges, it's time to press pause and peer into the underbelly of your spending habits. Understanding what triggers your wallet to open is the first critical step in reshaping your financial landscape. Let's dissect the three common triggers: emotional spending, environmental influences, and peer pressure, to help you gain control and pave the way to a wealthier lifestyle.

HACK 55- Emotional Spending

It's been a long day; you're feeling down and out. The lure of retail therapy whispers, promising a quick fix to elevate your mood. Sounds familiar? Emotional spending is one of the most common yet overlooked triggers that can wreak havoc on your finances. This phenomenon occurs when you buy items not out of necessity but as a way to manage your emotions.

To tackle this, start by observing your emotional states before and after purchases. Do you tend to shop more when you're feeling stressed, bored, or upset? Keeping a 'mood and spending' diary can be an eye-opener. Write down how you felt before buying something, what you bought, and how you felt afterwards. Over time, patterns will emerge.

Once you identify your emotional triggers, you can begin to address them more healthily. For instance, if stress drives you to online shopping, consider alternative stress-relief techniques such as yoga, a walk in the park, or even meditating for a few minutes. The key is to replace the temporary high of spending with activities that provide lasting satisfaction without financial repercussions.

HACK 56- Environmental Influences

Your surroundings play a critical role in shaping your spending habits. From flashy advertisements and the convenience of online shopping platforms to the well-placed impulse buy items in supermarkets, environmental cues can significantly influence your spending behavior.

To become more resistant to these cues, start by streamlining your exposure. Unsubscribe from marketing emails and unfollow brands on social media that tempt you to spend unnecessarily. When shopping, especially in supermarkets or malls, stick to the peripheries where essential items are typically located, and the middle aisles where more impulse items are placed are avoided.

Moreover, consider the setup of your home. Is it arranged in a way that encourages spending? For instance, storing your credit cards in easily accessible places can make impulsive online shopping all too easy. Try rearranging your environment to support frugal habits, such as keeping your credit cards out of sight and linking your online shopping accounts to a debit card with limited funds.

HACK 57- Peer Pressure

It's human nature to want to fit in, but this can often lead to spending money you don't have, to impress people you might not even like. Whether it's splashing out on the latest tech gadgets because your friends have them, or attending every group outing despite the dent it puts in your wallet, peer pressure is a potent trigger.

Dealing with this trigger involves setting healthy financial boundaries and learning to say no. Start by evaluating your social activities and identify which ones are pushing you beyond your financial comfort zone. It's okay to opt out of expensive gatherings or suggest alternative activities that are more budget-friendly. True friends will understand and respect your financial goals.

Additionally, spend time with people who share your financial values. This alignment can reinforce your resolve and help keep you on track. Remember, wealth isn't about flaunting expensive items but building a secure and comfortable future.

By understanding these triggers—emotional spending, environmental influences, and peer pressure—you can begin to dismantle the habits that lead to unnecessary spending. Take control of your financial journey by recognizing these triggers and actively choosing to manage them in a way that aligns with your aspirations for a richer life. Remember, the goal is not merely to spend less but to spend smart and save more for the future you envision.

Breaking Bad Habits

Let's dive straight into the thick of things, shall we? Once you've identified your triggers for problem spending, the next logical step is to tackle these habits head-on. It's about creating new, healthier financial routines that not only challenge your current spending patterns but also set you on a clearer path to financial freedom. Ready to break bad? Let's get started.

HACK 58- Shopping Lists and Budgets

Imagine walking into a supermarket with a clear list in your hand. You breeze past aisles of unnecessary temptations, focused solely on what you came for. That's the power of the humble shopping list. It's not just about groceries, though. This principle applies to all areas of spending.

Creating a shopping list for every expenditure, big or small, introduces a layer of accountability. It forces you to think critically about what you really need versus what is merely a fleeting want. Before any purchase, ask yourself: "Is this item on my list?" If not, why do you suddenly feel the need to buy it? This simple question can help curb impulse buys, keeping your spending in check.

But a list is only as powerful as the budget backing it. Budgeting might sound like a chore, but think of it as your financial roadmap. Start by tracking every penny you spend for a month— yes, even that cheeky coffee on the way to work. Once you have a clear view of where your money is going, categorize your spending. How much goes into necessities versus luxuries?

From here, set realistic limits for each category. Use tools like budgeting apps or spreadsheets to keep you in line. Remember, a budget is not set in stone; it's a living document that should adapt to your changing financial landscape. The key here is consistency. Stick with it, and you'll start to see where you can cut back without feeling restricted.

HACK 59- Cash-only Challenges

Now, let's turn up the notch a bit with a cash-only challenge. It's exactly what it sounds like: for a set period, you use only cash for all your transactions. No debit cards, no credit cards, just good old-fashioned currency.

Why bother, you ask? Because when you see actual cash leaving your hands, it feels more real than tapping a piece of plastic. It's psychological—harder to part with physical money than to swipe a card carelessly. This tactic helps you visualize your spending in a tangible way.

Start with a week, and see how you fare. Withdraw a predetermined amount of cash that aligns with your weekly budget and use it to cover all your expenses. It might sound daunting, but you'll likely find yourself thinking twice about each purchase, evaluating its necessity more critically.

One tip: divide your cash into envelopes, each labeled for a different spending category like groceries, transport, or entertainment. Once an envelope is empty, that's it for spending in that category for the week. It's a stark, effective way to keep your spending under control.

HACK 60- Mindful Spending Practices

Finally, let's talk about mindful spending. This isn't about cutting out all joys and living like a hermit. Rather, it's about making more informed, deliberate choices that align with your long-term financial goals.

Start by reflecting on each purchase. How does buying this item benefit you? Does it bring you joy or utility, or is it merely a momentary high? Sometimes, just pausing to think before buying can be incredibly powerful.

Another part of mindful spending is understanding the difference between cost and value. A cheap item that breaks down after a few uses is more expensive in the long run than a higher-quality product that lasts for years. Learn to assess the true value of a product beyond its price tag.

Additionally, consider the concept of 'opportunity cost'. Spending money on this item now means you have less money for something else later. Is the trade-off worth it? What could you achieve if you saved this money instead?

Incorporate these practices into your daily routine, and soon, they'll become second nature. You'll find yourself making smarter, more deliberate choices that not only save you money but also contribute to a healthier financial lifestyle.

By adopting these strategies—making and sticking to shopping lists and budgets, challenging yourself with cash-only periods, and practicing mindful spending—you're not just cutting costs; you're cultivating habits that pave the way to a richer, more fulfilling life. Remember, it's not about deprivation but about making smarter choices that align with your financial goals and aspirations. So, take control, challenge yourself, and transform your relationship with money.

Long-term Behavioral Changes

HACK 61- Financial Literacy Education

Embarking on a journey towards financial literacy is akin to learning a new language. It might seem daunting at first, but once you grasp the basics, you'll find yourself navigating through the world of finance with greater ease and confidence. Financial literacy isn't just about understanding how money works; it's about making money work for you.

Firstly, you need to get comfortable with the core concepts of personal finance, including budgeting, investing, saving, and debt management. Numerous online platforms offer free courses that can help elevate your understanding from novice to savvy spender. Websites like the Money Advice Service or FutureLearn offer user-friendly courses that cover everything from basic budgeting skills to investment strategies.

Moreover, reading books can be remarkably enlightening. Opt for titles that break down complex financial concepts into digestible pieces. Books like "The Financial Diet" by Chelsea Fagan and Lauren Ver Hage or "Rich Dad Poor Dad" by Robert Kiyosaki provide practical advice in an engaging manner.

Remember, the goal of enhancing your financial literacy is not just to accumulate wealth but to develop the ability to make informed and effective decisions about the use of your financial resources. This knowledge isn't just a tool for building wealth; it's your shield against financial misinformation and pitfalls.

HACK 62- Setting Long-term Financial Goals

Long-term financial goals are not just aspirations but destinations you plan to reach through the landscape of your financial journey. These goals could range from buying a home, saving for retirement, or setting up a college fund for your children. The clarity of these goals acts as a motivator and a navigator, helping you stay focused and steer clear of unnecessary detours.

To start setting these goals, visualize where you want to be in five, ten, or even twenty years. What do you see? Does it include owning a home free of mortgage, traveling the world, or perhaps enjoying a comfortable retirement? Once you have a clear picture, break these down into smaller, actionable steps. For instance, if your goal is to purchase a home, figure out how much you need for a down payment and start saving towards that.

One effective method to stay on track is the SMART criteria—

ensure your goals are Specific, Measurable, Achievable, Relevant, and Time-bound. A goal articulated as, "I want to save £20,000 for a down payment in five years," meets all these criteria and is more likely to be achieved than a vague "I want to buy a house someday."

Additionally, leverage tools that can help keep your goals in sight. Budgeting apps can track your progress, and regular financial reviews, say every six months, can help adjust your plans as needed. Remember, the journey towards significant financial milestones is a marathon, not a sprint; persistence and patience are your allies.

HACK 63- Seeking Support Groups

The path to financial stability and literacy is often rugged and can feel lonely. However, you don't have to walk this path alone. Engaging with a community of like-minded individuals can provide not only moral support but also a wealth of shared knowledge and experiences.

Support groups, whether online or in your local community, can be instrumental. These groups provide a platform to learn from others' successes and setbacks and to gain insights that are not readily available in books or online courses. For instance, a member of your group might know the ins and outs of investing in local real estate, or another might offer tips on cutting down everyday expenses without sacrificing quality of life.

Platforms like Meetup often host groups focused on personal finance and investing. Online forums and social media groups also offer spaces where questions can be asked and wisdom shared freely and without judgment. Engaging in these communities allows you to gain diverse perspectives, encouraging holistic growth in your financial journey.

Moreover, don't underestimate the value of accountability that comes with being part of such groups. Just knowing that you're expected to share your progress can spur you to stick more closely to your financial goals. It's about creating a positive pressure that propels you forward.

In embracing these long-term behavioral changes, you are not just altering your immediate financial landscape but are paving the way for a future where financial stability and freedom are not just dreams, but achievable realities. Remember, every small step taken in education, goal-setting, and community engagement is a foundational block towards building a wealthier, more secure financial future.

RECAP AND ACTION ITEMS ON THE

9 PROBLEM SPENDING HACKS

By now, you've taken a deep dive into the roots of problem spending, equipped yourself with strategies to break those pesky habits, and laid out a blueprint for sustaining healthy financial behaviors. The journey toward a richer life isn't necessarily about earning more money, but about optimizing how you manage what you have. It's about making money work for you, not the other way around.

Let's wrap up what you've learned and jump into some concrete steps you can take today:

Recognize Your Triggers:

You've explored emotional spending, environmental influences, and peer pressure. Keep a spending diary for the next month. Each time you make a purchase, jot down what triggered it. Was it a bad day at work? A flashy advertisement? Or perhaps pressure from friends to keep up? Understanding these triggers is your first defense against needless spending.

Implement Break Strategies:

Start with the shopping list and budget approach. Before you go shopping, write down what you need and stick to it. Try the cash-only challenge for a week: withdraw a fixed amount of money for your expenses and leave your cards at home. It's a tactile way to feel your spending. Lastly, engage in mindful spending by asking yourself if this purchase is a need or a want. If it's a want, what emotion are you trying to satisfy?

Cultivate Sustainable Habits:

Knowledge is power. Enroll in a financial literacy course or pick up a book on personal finance. Set clear, achievable financial goals for the next year, five years, and ten years. Visualize where you want to be and break down the steps to get there. Finally, don't underestimate the power of community. Join a support group or find a money management buddy. Sharing your goals and struggles can make them much easier to navigate.

Remember, every big change starts with a series of small ones. Don't beat yourself up over occasional slip-ups. Acknowledge them, learn from them, and move forward. With these tools and strategies, you're well on your way to a wealthier and more fulfilling lifestyle. Keep pushing, keep learning, and let your budget be your guide, not your boundary.

8

BUILDING FINANCIAL RESILIENCE

"It is not the strongest of the species that survive, nor the most intelligent, but the one most responsive to change." - Charles Darwin

Emergency Preparedness

Life has a knack for throwing curveballs when you least expect them. While we can't predict every twist and turn, we can certainly prepare for many of the financial storms that might come our way. Think of financial resilience as your personal buffer against life's uncertainties—like an invisible shield that keeps you safe when things get rough. In this section, we're diving into the essentials of emergency preparedness. You'll learn how to build a robust rainy day fund, understand the ins and outs of necessary insurance, and discover strategies to disaster-proof your finances. Let's get you set up so that no matter what life throws at you, you're ready to face it head-on.

HACK 64- Creating a Rainy Day Fund

The cornerstone of financial resilience is undoubtedly the rainy day fund. This is your financial backstop that keeps you afloat when sudden expenses strike. So, how much should you save? A good rule of thumb is to have at least three to six months' worth of living expenses tucked away. But let's break that down into actionable steps, so it doesn't seem like such a mountain to climb.

Firstly, assess your monthly expenses. Include everything from rent or mortgage payments, utility bills, groceries, and transport, to any recurring subscriptions. Once you have a clear picture, aim to save a portion of your income each month to build up this fund. Even starting small can make a difference. If saving a large chunk of your income isn't feasible right now, don't sweat it. Begin with maybe 5% of your monthly income, and gradually increase this as you can.

The key is consistency. Set up a direct debit from your checking account to a savings account dedicated solely to your emergency fund. This makes your saving effort automatic and painless. Choose a high-interest savings account where your money can grow while it sits, making your fund work harder for you.

HACK 65- Insurance Essentials

Insurance might not be the most thrilling of topics, but understanding it and having the right coverages in place can save you a world of financial pain. Think of insurance as a small price you pay for big peace of mind. But what types of insurance are crucial?

Health Insurance:

This is paramount. Medical emergencies can happen without warning, and the costs can be staggering. Ensure you have a policy that covers your basic health needs and any specific conditions you might have

Home Insurance:

Whether you own or rent, protecting your dwelling place and belongings from damage or theft is crucial. If you own your home, consider a comprehensive policy that covers both the structure and the contents. If you're renting, contents insurance can protect your personal belongings.

Car Insurance:

It's not just a legal necessity; it's a financial safety net. Depending on your vehicle and budget, consider if third-party or comprehensive coverage best suits your needs.

Life Insurance:

Especially important if you have dependents. It ensures that in the event of your passing, your loved ones have financial support.

Take the time to shop around for insurance. Compare policies not just on price, but on what coverage they offer. Check reviews and ratings of insurance providers to ensure they pay out when needed. Remember, cheapest isn't always best when it comes to insurance.

HACK 66- Disaster-Proofing Your Finances

Finally, let's talk about fortifying your financial landscape against potential disasters. This isn't just about having savings or insurance; it's about creating a holistic strategy that keeps you financially secure no matter what.

Diversify Your Income:

Relying on a single income source can be risky. Consider exploring side hustles or passive income streams that can bolster your earnings.

Keep Your Debt in Check:

High levels of debt can cripple your financial stability. Aim to keep your debt manageable, focus on paying off high-interest debts first, and use credit wisely.

Stay Informed:

Keep yourself updated with financial news and trends. Knowledge is power, and understanding the economic environment can help you make informed decisions about your investments and savings.

Plan for the Long Term:

Regularly review your financial plan. Are your investments aligned with your future goals? Are you saving enough for retirement? Adjust your plan as necessary to stay on track.

Emergency Contacts and Documents:

Ensure that all your important financial documents are safe and accessible. Keep a list of emergency contacts, including your financial advisor, insurance agent, and family members who should be informed about your financial affairs in an emergency.

Building financial resilience isn't about overhauling your life overnight. It's about taking thoughtful, consistent steps to safeguard your financial future. By setting up a solid rainy day fund, ensuring you have adequate insurance, and disaster-proofing your finances, you're not just surviving; you're thriving, no matter what challenges come your way.

Navigating Financial Setbacks

HACK 67- Handling Job Loss or Income Reduction

It's a scenario that can knock the wind out of your sails: job loss or an unexpected reduction in income. Maybe it's a downturn in the market, a company restructuring, or a sudden personal setback. Whatever the cause, the impact on your financial life can feel devastating. But here's the kicker—it's also an opportunity to transform your approach to money management and emerge stronger.

First, take a deep breath. Panic is a natural reaction, but it won't be your ally here. Start by reassessing your budget. This isn't just about cutting back—though that's part of it—it's about smarter allocation of funds. Prioritize essentials like rent, utilities, and food. Non-essentials? They're on pause. It's time to embody the art of frugality.

Next, communicate openly with anyone who might be impacted by your financial shift—this could include family members or anyone dependent on your income. Transparency can prevent misunderstandings and shared responsibility can lighten the load.

Now, explore all avenues for financial support. This might mean applying for unemployment benefits, seeking temporary work, or even tapping into community resources designed for such times. Every little helps, and pride should not prevent you from accessing available help.

Remember, restructuring your career isn't just about finding the next job—it's about finding the right job. Use this time to upskill. Online courses, workshops, and books can equip you with new skills that might open doors in fields you hadn't considered before.

HACK 68- Dealing with Unexpected Expenses

No matter how well you plan, life has a knack for throwing curveballs. The boiler breaks in mid-winter, the car conks out on the way to an important meeting, or a family emergency pulls you across the country—or even the globe. These are the moments when having a strategy can make a world of difference.

Firstly, if you haven't yet encountered a major unexpected expense, start preparing now. This ties back to the importance of a rainy day fund, which should ideally cover three to six months of living expenses. If you're starting from scratch, aim to set aside a small, manageable amount each month. It might be the equivalent of a night out or a weekend getaway, but over time, it adds up.

When the inevitable happens, evaluate the necessity and urgency of the expense. Is it something that needs immediate attention, or can it wait until you have more financial flexibility? If it's urgent, shopping around for the best deal or negotiating payment terms can reduce the burden.

For larger, more daunting costs, consider speaking to your bank about a short-term loan or a credit line increase. Yes, debt is generally something to avoid, but in emergencies, accessing credit can sometimes be a necessary evil—and a well-negotiated deal can minimize the long-term cost.

HACK 69- Rebounding from Financial Mistakes

Everyone makes mistakes, but not everyone learns from them. Financial blunders, while painful, are rich with lessons. Maybe you invested in a 'sure thing' that wasn't, or perhaps impulse purchases have left you with a mountain of debt. Here's how you can turn those mistakes into masterclasses in personal finance.

First off, acknowledge the mistake. Ownership is empowering and the first step towards not repeating history. Analyze what went wrong. Was it a lack of research? Peer pressure? A misunderstanding of your own financial limits? Identifying the root cause can prevent a repeat performance.

Next, create a recovery plan. If it's debt you're dealing with, assess all your debts together—interest rates, monthly payments, total amounts—and start with the most pressing ones. Techniques like the debt snowball method (paying off debts from smallest to largest) can create momentum and help keep you motivated.

For investment flops, consider consulting a financial advisor to understand better strategies. Investing isn't about winning every time; it's about strategic wins and manageable losses. Diversification is often key to a healthier investment portfolio.

Lastly, keep the big picture in mind. Financial resilience isn't built in a day. Each setback is a stepping stone to a more secure financial future. Incremental changes, consistent efforts, and a commitment to learning from the past are what will define your financial narrative.

Navigating financial setbacks isn't just about weathering storms—it's about learning to dance in the rain. By embracing these strategies, you're not just surviving; you're setting the stage for a future where financial setbacks have less impact on your peace and prosperity. Keep pushing forward, keep learning, and remember, resilience is a journey, not a destination.

Strengthening Financial Health

HACK 70- Boosting Financial Literacy

The journey to a richer life starts with understanding the nuts and bolts of your finances. Think about it: you wouldn't try to build a house without knowing how to use the tools, right? The same goes for building your wealth. Financial literacy is your toolbox for making informed decisions and navigating the complex world of money.

Start by getting to grips with the basics: budgeting, saving, and the principles of investing. Knowing how to manage your monthly income and expenses creates a solid foundation for all your financial decisions. But don't stop there; dive deeper into understanding credit scores, how mortgages work, and the implications of different types of loans. Knowledge is power – the more you know, the better equipped you are to make decisions that align with your long-term financial goals.

To really enhance your financial literacy, make learning a regular part of your routine. Follow financial news, read books by financial experts, and perhaps most importantly, talk to professionals. Financial advisors, for example, can offer personalized advice that considers your individual circumstances. Remember, the goal here is not just to accumulate information but to understand how to apply this knowledge to your financial strategies.

HACK 71- Developing Multiple Income Streams

Relying solely on your 9-5 job for income is a bit like putting all your eggs in one basket — risky and limiting. In today's gig economy, creating multiple income streams is not just smart; it's necessary for financial resilience.

Start with your passions and skills. What do you love doing that you can monetize? Perhaps you have a knack for graphic design, writing, or crafting—these can all be turned into freelance opportunities. Online platforms like Etsy, Upwork, and Fiverr make it easier than ever to market your skills to a global audience.

If you're not keen on trading more of your time for money, consider passive income streams. These could be investments in stocks or real estate that pay dividends or rental income. Alternatively, you might create a product, such as an eBook or an online course, that requires a lot of upfront effort but then generates income over time with little additional work.

It's important to note that developing new income streams might require an initial investment of time and money. However, the financial security they can provide makes them well worth the effort. Diversifying your income can help cushion you against job loss, reduce financial stress, and ultimately give you the freedom to pursue your passions.

HACK 72- Maintaining Financial Flexibility

Financial flexibility is about having the ability to adapt to changes and seize opportunities as they arise. It's a crucial aspect of financial health, especially in unpredictable times.

One key component of maintaining financial flexibility is keeping your fixed expenses low. These are your regular, unavoidable bills—think rent, utilities, and subscriptions. The lower these are, the more of your income you can allocate to savings and investments, or use to pivot when a great opportunity comes along.

Another aspect of financial flexibility involves having access to emergency funds. This isn't just about having a rainy day fund (which you should definitely have!), but also about ensuring you can access your money when you need it. This might mean choosing savings accounts with no withdrawal penalties, or keeping some of your investments in more liquid forms, like certain stocks or bonds.

Lastly, stay proactive about reducing debt. High-interest debt, especially from credit cards, can quickly eat into your financial flexibility. Prioritize paying off high-interest debts and consider consolidating debts to lower interest rates if possible. Not only does this free up more of your money on a monthly basis, but it also improves your credit score, which can be crucial for financial maneuverability.

By enhancing your financial literacy, developing multiple income streams, and maintaining financial flexibility, you are not just surviving; you're setting the stage to thrive. Each step you take builds more strength into your financial structure, making it resilient enough to withstand setbacks and agile enough to capitalize on opportunities. Remember, the goal here is to build a wealthier lifestyle, not just for today, but for the long haul. So, keep learning, keep diversifying, and keep your options open. Your future self will thank you.

RECAP AND ACTION ITEMS ON THE

9 BUILDING FINANCIAL RESILIENCE HACKS

You've just armed yourself with a toolkit to build financial resilience, a crucial step towards a richer, more secure lifestyle. Let's quickly recap the essentials and then leap into some actionable steps you can take immediately.

Firstly, emergency preparedness is your financial safety net. You've learned the importance of establishing a rainy day fund, ensuring adequate insurance coverage, and disaster-proofing your finances. These are your shields against the unexpected blows that life might throw your way.

Next, we navigated through the rough waters of financial setbacks. Handling job loss or income reduction, dealing with unexpected expenses, and rebounding from financial mistakes are all part of the journey. Remember, setbacks are not roadblocks but detours that can lead to new paths of financial growth and stability.

Lastly, strengthening your financial health by boosting financial literacy, developing multiple income streams, and maintaining financial flexibility ensures that you are not just surviving, but thriving. These strategies are about building a robust financial structure that supports your life goals and dreams.

Now, onto the action steps:

Start Your Emergency Fund:

Open a savings account if you don't already have one and set up an automatic transfer for each payday. Even a small amount, like £50 or £100, can start your journey towards financial security.

Review Your Insurance Needs:

Make a list of your current insurance policies and assess if they adequately cover your current lifestyle. If not, it's time to shop around or speak to an insurance advisor.

Audit Your Expenses:

Go through your last three months' bank statements. Identify any unexpected expenses and think about how you could handle these better in the future. This could mean setting aside a little extra in your emergency fund or cutting unnecessary spending.

Educate Yourself Financially:

Pick one financial topic you feel you should know more about. This could be investments, retirement planning, or even just budgeting. Spend an hour each week educating yourself through books, podcasts, or online courses.

Explore Additional Income Streams:

Brainstorm five ways you could potentially generate additional income. These could range from freelancing, investing in stocks, starting a small side business, or using any particular skills you have. Evaluate these and aim to start one within the next six months.

Flex Your Financial Flexibility:

Practice saying no to non-essential expenses for a month. This could strengthen your spending discipline and help enhance your financial flexibility.

By integrating these steps into your life, you're not just dreaming of a wealthier lifestyle; you're actively constructing it. Each action you take builds a stronger financial foundation, ensuring that when storms come — and they will — you'll stand firm. Keep pushing forward, and remember, resilience is built one step at a time.

9

PAVING THE PATH TO RETIREMENT

"Someone's sitting in the shade today because someone planted a tree a long time ago." - Warren Buffett

Early Planning Perks

HACK 73- Understanding Pensions

Let's kick off with something a bit less glamorous but absolutely crucial: pensions. Think of your pension as a paycheck in your golden years, a reward for all the hard work you've put in. Getting to grips with pensions now can transform your future self's lifestyle.

In the UK, you've got a few types of pensions to wrap your head around: the State Pension, provided by the government; occupational pensions, which are organized through your employer; and personal or stakeholder pensions, which you set up yourself. Each type serves its own purpose, and understanding the nuances can maximize your retirement income.

Firstly, the State Pension acts as a foundation. To qualify, you need at least 10 years on your National Insurance record, but for the full amount, you're looking at 35 years. It's a solid base, but rarely enough to live comfortably on its own.

This is where occupational pensions come into play. If your employer offers a pension scheme, they usually match your contributions to some extent. It's like getting free money for your future self, so always aim to maximize what you put in if your budget allows.

Personal pensions give you the most control. You choose the provider and how much you invest. It's a fantastic option if you're self-employed or want to supplement other pension pots. Remember, the government tops up your contributions in the form of tax relief, making them even more worthwhile.

HACK 74- The Power of Compound Interest

Now, onto the magic of compound interest – it's the secret sauce that can make your money grow exponentially over time. Imagine planting a tree. Initially, growth is slow, but over many years, that tree becomes a robust, sprawling entity. That's how compound interest works with your savings.

Here's a simple way to look at it: when you invest money, it earns interest. The next year, you earn interest on both your initial sum and the interest from the first year, and so on. Over 20, 30, or 40 years, that amount can grow massively.

To truly benefit from compound interest, start as early as possible. Even small amounts can snowball into substantial sums over long periods. Let's say you start saving £200 a month at 25, with an average annual interest rate of 5%. By the time you hit 65, you'd have over £245,000. But if you start at 35, you'd accumulate about £140,000 under the same conditions. That's a massive difference just by starting ten years earlier!

HACK 75- Retirement Age Calculations

Determining when you can retire isn't just about picking an age when you'd like to stop working. It involves some number crunching and realistic planning. Consider how long you will need to fund your retirement. People are living longer, often into their 80s and 90s, so your retirement pot needs to last.

Start by envisioning your ideal retirement lifestyle. Do you see yourself traveling, indulging in hobbies, or moving to the countryside? Each scenario costs a different amount. -Once you have a rough idea, backtrack to see how much you need to save each month to reach that goal.

Use online retirement calculators as a starting point to estimate how much you need to stash away. These tools consider your current age, savings rate, and desired retirement age to give you a ballpark figure of your required contributions.

Also, think about the age you can start drawing from your pension without penalty. For most private pensions, it's currently 55, but this is scheduled to rise to 57 in 2028. The State Pension age is also increasing and is expected to rise as life expectancy increases. Keeping up to date with these changes is crucial as they could significantly impact your plans.

Retirement planning isn't just about surviving; it's about thriving. Starting early affords you the flexibility to adjust your plans and take advantage of opportunities as they arise, whether that's investing more aggressively when you can afford to or scaling back when other life costs like raising children or buying a home take priority.

By tackling these three aspects of early retirement planning, you're not just preparing financially; you're setting the stage for a richer, more fulfilling life post-work. Remember, a little foresight now makes all the difference later. Start today, and pave your path to a comfortable, enjoyable retirement.

Investment Strategies for the Future

When you're looking at padding your nest egg, there's more to it than just stashing away chunks of your salary. It's about smart, savvy investment strategies that not only preserve but also grow your wealth over time. Let's dive into three fundamental pillars:

Diversification, Risk Assessment, and Tax-efficient Investing.

HACK 76- Diversification

Imagine investing as if you're planning a well-rounded diet. Just as you wouldn't rely solely on apples for nutrition, you shouldn't depend on just one kind of investment to grow your wealth. Diversification is your financial fiber – essential and often overlooked.

To start, think of diversification as spreading your investment risks across various financial instruments, industries, and other categories. It's about creating a portfolio where your assets don't all dance to the same tune. When the stock market dips, perhaps the bonds hold steady or even appreciate. If real estate is sluggish, maybe your tech stocks are having a rally.

But how do you begin to diversify? Start with the basics: stocks, bonds, and cash are fundamental categories. Yet, within each category, the diversity must continue. International stocks can complement domestic ones, government bonds can balance corporate ones, and so on.

Remember, though, diversification doesn't mean throwing your money at every available opportunity. It's about finding the right balance that aligns with your financial goals and risk tolerance. This leads seamlessly into our next pillar.

HACK 77- Risk Assessment

Risk is not a dirty word. It's a reality in the investment world that you need to understand and embrace to a degree that suits you. Risk assessment is about knowing how much volatility you can handle without losing sleep. It's okay to be cautious, but too much caution can be as detrimental as recklessness.

Start by assessing your current financial situation and your future financial needs. Consider factors such as your age, your income, your financial responsibilities, and when you plan to retire. Younger investors might opt for higher-risk (and potentially higher-return) investments since they have time to recover from any downturns. However, if you're closer to retirement, you might prefer more conservative investments.

Also, consider your emotional risk tolerance. Are you the type who watches the stock ticker daily, fretting over every dip? Or do you prefer to set your investments and check on them occasionally? Understanding your emotional response to risk will help you build a portfolio that doesn't cause undue stress.

Tools like risk tolerance questionnaires can be extremely useful. Financial advisors often use these tools, but there are also versions available online. They can help you quantify your risk tolerance and see where you fit on the risk spectrum.

HACK 78- Tax-efficient Investing

No one likes to give a sizable chunk of their returns back to the taxman. Tax-efficient investing is about keeping more of what you earn by taking advantage of tax breaks and choosing the right investment vehicles.

One of the first places to look is your Individual Savings Account (ISA). You can contribute up to a certain limit each year, and the returns you earn from an ISA are tax-free. It's a fantastic way to save money without worrying about capital gains tax or dividend tax.

Pensions are another critical area. Contributions to your pension can reduce your taxable income, and the investment growth in a pension is tax-free. Plus, you get some tax-free cash when you finally draw your pension. It's a triple win for tax efficiency.

Beyond ISAs and pensions, consider how the timing of buying and selling investments can affect your tax liability. Capital gains tax can take a bite out of your profits if you're not careful. One strategy is to use your capital gains tax allowance each year. By realizing gains in a controlled manner, you can potentially reduce the amount of tax payable.

Also, think about the location of your investments. Different types of investments are taxed differently. For example, dividends from shares might be taxed at a different rate than interest from bonds. Understanding these nuances can help you make smarter choices that minimize your tax burden.

In conclusion, weaving these strategies into your investment plan isn't just about growing your wealth; it's about protecting it, nurturing it, and making it work efficiently for your future. By diversifying your investments, assessing your risk tolerance, and optimizing for tax efficiency, you're setting yourself up not just for a richer tomorrow, but a smarter, more secure financial future.

Lifestyle Adjustments for Later Life

HACK 79- Downsizing Options

Imagine a life where every square foot of your home is not just a place you clean, but a space you use and enjoy. As retirement beckons, the concept of downsizing can be not just beneficial but essential for a more streamlined and stress-free lifestyle. It's not merely about moving to a smaller space—it's about optimizing your living situation to enhance your quality of life.

Downsizing might mean trading a large family home for a more manageable flat or bungalow. This transition isn't just about physical ease (less cleaning and maintenance!), but also financial relief. The costs associated with a larger home can be substantial—from higher energy bills to greater council taxes and maintenance expenses. By choosing a smaller home, you could free up equity from your current property and reduce ongoing expenses, boosting your disposable income for better uses like travel or hobbies.

Moreover, think about the location. Perhaps a city Center, with easy access to amenities like healthcare, entertainment, and public transport, could offer a more vibrant lifestyle than a secluded suburban home. Or maybe a community designed for retirees, which often comes with added perks like security, maintenance services, and social activities to keep you engaged and active.

HACK 80- Passive Income Streams

Retirement might signal the end of a nine-to-five job, but it doesn't mean the end of income opportunities. Establishing passive income streams is like setting up a series of small taps that can keep the flow of money trickling in without the constant effort.

One popular route is investing in rental properties. If managed wisely, properties can provide a steady income well into retirement. However, being a landlord isn't everyone's cup of tea—dealing with tenants and maintenance can be a hassle. So, consider property management companies that can take care of the day-to-day responsibilities. Yes, they charge a fee, but the trade-off for hassle-free income might just be worth it.

Another avenue is investing in stocks that pay dividends. Unlike regular stocks, which bring in income through price appreciation, dividend stocks pay regular portions of the company's profits to shareholders. These can be reinvested or used as a steady income stream. It's a powerful way to benefit from the economic growth without selling your investments.

Alternatively, think about capitalizing on a hobby or skill. Whether it's crafting, photography, or writing, the digital age offers myriad platforms to turn your passion into profit. Online marketplaces, blogs, or tutorial channels can all be sources of income that you can manage from the comfort of your home at your own pace.

HACK 81- Health Care Planning

As much as we might hate to admit it, our health needs tend to increase as we age. Effective health care planning is crucial to ensure that these golden years remain bright and aren't overshadowed by stress and uncertainty about medical issues.

Firstly, consider your options for health insurance. If you've been relying on an employer's plan, retirement may require shifting gears. Look into what the NHS offers and whether getting a private health insurance could provide you with quicker access to treatment and more medical services. It's also wise to compare different plans and consider factors like coverage, exclusions, and premiums.

Secondly, think about your proximity to medical facilities when choosing where to live. Being relatively close to a good hospital or clinic can reduce stress and travel time during medical emergencies. Also, check if the area has reliable transportation options for those days when driving might not be an option.

Lastly, maintain a healthy lifestyle. Regular exercise, a balanced diet, and mental health care are pillars that can keep you robust. Consider joining clubs or groups that engage in physical activities you enjoy—be it yoga, walking, or swimming. Such communities not only help you keep fit but also keep you socially engaged, which is equally vital for mental health.

By integrating these adjustments into your lifestyle, you're not just planning for retirement; you're setting the stage for a vibrant, fulfilling, and secure phase of life. Each step you take towards downsizing, developing passive income, and planning your healthcare not only secures your future but also enriches your present, letting you thrive in these golden years.

RECAP AND ACTION ITEMS ON THE

9 PAVING THE PATH TO RETIREMENT HACKS

You've just navigated through a wealth of information that can transform your approach to retirement, making it not just a distant dream but a feasible, well-planned reality. Let's cement these concepts with practical steps you can take to start paving your path to a richer retirement today.

Firstly, delve deeper into understanding your pension options.

Whether it's a company pension, a private pension, or state benefits, get clear on what you're entitled to and how you can maximize these funds. Make an appointment with a financial advisor or use online tools to get a solid grasp of your projected income at retirement.

Next, harness the power of compound interest. Start by reviewing your current savings and investment accounts. Are they offering you the best return? If not, it's time to shop around. Consider setting up automatic transfers to your savings account right after payday; it's an easy way to ensure you consistently invest in your future.

Additionally, refine your retirement age calculations. Use online calculators to play around with different scenarios. How does retiring earlier affect your pension payouts? What about later? Understanding these dynamics can help you plan more effectively, aligning your retirement age with your lifestyle goals and financial possibilities.

Moving on to investment strategies, begin by evaluating your current portfolio. Is it diversified enough to mitigate risks while giving you the best possible returns? If you're unsure, this might be another good moment to consult a financial advisor.

Risk assessment is crucial. Review your investments in terms of risk versus return. Are you comfortable with your current balance? Your risk tolerance might change as you get closer to retirement, so keep this in review.

Tax-efficient investing is your next focal point. Ensure you're making the most of ISAs, pensions, and other tax-efficient vehicles. Familiarize yourself with the latest tax laws and benefits that could affect your investments, potentially saving you a substantial amount in taxes over time.

Finally, consider lifestyle adjustments. If downsizing seems like a viable option, start researching smaller homes or locations with a lower cost of living. This could free up cash for other investments that can generate passive income.

Speaking of passive income, explore avenues that require minimal effort but promise steady returns, like dividend stocks or rental properties. And don't forget about planning for healthcare. Investigate insurance plans and health savings accounts that could cover future medical costs, keeping you financially secure in your later years.

By taking these steps, you're not just planning; you're actively securing a wealthier, more comfortable retirement. The path is clear, and every small action you take now is a significant leap towards that richer life you aspire to. Remember, the best time to start was yesterday; the next best time is today.

10

CRAFTING YOUR LEGACY

"The greatest use of a life is to spend it on something that will outlast it." – *William James*

Estate Planning Essentials

When you hear the phrase "estate planning," your mind might conjure up images of affluent individuals with vast assets to distribute. However, stripping it back to basics, estate planning is just a methodical approach for anyone to ensure their financial affairs are in order, no matter the size of their estate. It's about making sure that what you've worked hard for ends up in the right hands and that your loved ones are cared for in the way you intend. Let's break down the essentials: writing a will, setting up trusts, and choosing executors.

HACK 82- Writing a Will

The cornerstone of any solid estate plan is writing a will. Think of a will like the master plan of your legacy—it outlines who gets what and who oversees the distribution (more on executors later). Without one, you're leaving it up to laws and courts to decide where your assets go, which can often lead to unexpected and unwanted outcomes.

First off, let's debunk a myth: writing a will isn't just for the elderly. Life is unpredictable, and being prepared is key. The process doesn't have to be daunting. You can start simple. List out your assets—this includes your property, investments, and even those treasured personal items you know your niece loves. Next, decide who you want to inherit these assets. This could be family, friends, or even charities.

Legal advice can be invaluable here, especially if your situation has complexities like overseas properties or a blended family. However, for many, a straightforward will can be set up using reputable online services or templates guided by local laws. Just ensure it's legally binding, usually requiring witnesses or notarization depending on where you live.

HACK 83- Setting Up Trusts

Trusts might sound like high-finance concepts reserved for the one percent, but they're actually quite accessible and can be a smart tactic to manage how your assets are handled after you're gone. A trust is a legal entity where a trustee manages assets for the benefit of someone else—the beneficiary. Why set one up? Well, trusts can help reduce estate taxes, protect assets from creditors, and specify conditions under which assets are dispersed (like age conditions for younger family members).

There are various types of trusts, but let's focus on a simple revocable living trust, which is popular because you can change its terms at any point during your lifetime. This flexibility lets you adapt to life's changes—such as new members of the family or changes in your financial situation—without the rigidity of other legal structures.

You might use a trust to ensure your child's education is funded, or that a relative with special needs is provided for in a way that doesn't disrupt their eligibility for government benefits. Setting up a trust does usually require some legal legwork and upfront cost, but think of it as investing in peace of mind.

HACK 84- Choosing Executors

Finally, choosing an executor—this is the person who will carry out the wishes laid out in your will. It's a big role, encompassing everything from closing bank accounts to distributing assets. Therefore, it's crucial to choose someone who is not only trustworthy but also has the organizational skills to manage the tasks efficiently.

Often, people choose a close family member or a lifelong friend. However, it's also worth considering whether they might be too emotionally overwhelmed to perform the duties effectively. In some cases, appointing a professional, such as a solicitor or a dedicated estate executor, might be a better option. They may come with a fee, but their expertise can also provide reassurance that your estate is managed correctly.

Remember, the person you choose doesn't need to go it alone—they can hire professionals to help navigate the legal complexities. The important part is that they're capable of overseeing the process with the diligence and attention to detail it requires.

In conclusion, estate planning isn't just about preparing for the end; it's about maximizing the value of your life's work and ensuring that your loved ones are looked after. Whether it's through drafting a will, setting up a trust, or choosing the right executor, these steps empower you to control the narrative of your assets and the legacy you leave. Remember, estate planning is not a one-time task but an ongoing process that evolves with you. By taking control now, you make a profound investment in your family's future.

Financial Education for Your Family

HACK 85- Teaching Kids About Money

Let's dive right in—teaching kids about money is arguably one of the most powerful gifts you can give them. It's not just about saving pennies; it's about instilling a sense of responsibility, understanding, and foresight that can guide them throughout their lives.

Start simple. From as young as three or four, children can grasp basic concepts like counting and the value of different coins and notes. Introduce them to money through everyday activities. Next time you're at the shop, involve them in transactions. Let them hand over the money and receive the change. It's a practical demonstration of how transactions work.

As they grow, escalate the complexity. Give them a small allowance in exchange for chores. This isn't just about earning; it's about learning the value of work and the reward that comes with it. Encourage them to save a portion of their allowance. Maybe they're eyeing a new toy or a book; this is a perfect opportunity to teach about saving for goals.

But here's a crucial step: don't just tell them; show them. Consider opening a savings account for them and let them see their money grow. Most banks have accounts tailored for children that you can oversee. Discuss the statements with them, talk about interest, and explain how their money can increase over time through saving.

Moreover, introduce the concept of budgeting by setting up a simple system where they allocate their money for different purposes: savings, spending, and sharing. This can teach them about making choices and prioritizing their expenditures.

And remember, mistakes are part of the learning curve. If they blow their allowance on a whim, use that as a lesson about impulse spending and the importance of thoughtful purchases.

HACK 86- Creating Family Budgets

Now, let's talk about creating a family budget—a fantastic tool for managing your household's financial health and an excellent way for everyone to get involved in the financial dialogue.

First, gather all your financial statements: bills, bank statements, receipts, and any other records of income and expenditure. This will give you a clear picture of where money is coming from and where it's going.

Next, set up a family meeting. Yes, bring everyone into the conversation. Discuss what your family's financial goals are— be it saving for a holiday, buying a new car, or simply boosting your savings. Everyone's input is valuable, and when the whole family is involved, each member feels responsible for the outcome.

Outline all your income sources and monthly expenses. Categorize expenses as 'needs' (essentials like rent, food, utilities) and 'wants' (non-essentials like entertainment, dining out). This will help in understanding where you can potentially cut back.

Use tools to your advantage. A spreadsheet is a great way to visualize your budget, or you can use one of the many budgeting apps available. Track your spending regularly and review your budget together monthly. This not only helps in sticking to your budget but also in re-evaluating it regularly to suit changing needs.

Involving kids in this process can be particularly enlightening for them. It teaches them about the costs of everyday life and the importance of managing money wisely.

HACK 87- Involving Family in Financial Decisions

Involving your family in financial decisions is about creating a culture of transparency and shared responsibility. It's about making financial decisions as a unit that aligns with your collective long-term goals.

Start with setting financial goals together. Whether it's saving for education, a new family home, or retirement, make sure these goals are discussed and agreed upon by everyone. This not only ensures that everyone is on the same page but also makes it easier to work collectively towards these goals.

When it comes to investment decisions, educate and involve

your family in the discussions. If you're thinking of investing in stocks, bonds, or starting a new family business, discuss the potential benefits and risks involved. If your children are older, this might be the right time to introduce them to more complex financial concepts like the stock market or the principles of investing in real estate.

Consider regular family financial meetings to review your financial status and progress towards your goals. Use this time to discuss any major upcoming expenses or adjustments needed in your financial planning. It's also a great opportunity to address any financial concerns anyone might have.

Transparency is key. For instance, if facing financial hardship, instead of shielding your children completely, share appropriate details to foster understanding. This can help prepare them for real-life financial situations in the future.

By involving your family in these financial decisions, you're not just planning finances, you're also teaching valuable life lessons in teamwork, planning, and decision-making.

By embedding these practices—teaching kids about money, creating a family budget, and involving everyone in financial decisions—you're not just managing money, you're building a legacy of financial savvy and security that could benefit your family for generations to come.

Charitable Considerations

HACK 88- Choosing Charities

When you're looking at crafting a legacy that transcends financial wealth and delves into societal impact, selecting the right charities to support is a crucial step. It's not just about writing cheques to any organization that asks. It's about making smart, impactful choices that align with your values and the kind of change you want to see in the world.

Start by identifying causes that are close to your heart. Is it the environment, education, health, or community development? Narrowing down your focus to a specific sector can drastically increase the effectiveness of your contributions because it allows you to channel resources to where you feel they will make the most difference.

Once you've got your cause, it's time to vet the charities that work within that space. Look for transparency in operations and financial reporting. A trustworthy charity will have no qualities about sharing how they use donations, and their reports should be easily accessible to the public. Websites like Charity Navigator or The Charity Commission can provide insights into a charity's financial health, accountability, and transparency.

Understanding the impact of your chosen charity is also critical. How much of your donation goes directly to the cause? What tangible changes have they achieved with the funds? Check out their projects and look for qualitative as well as quantitative results. Sometimes, smaller, less well-known charities can make a massive impact in specific communities or sectors.

HACK 89- Planned Giving

Planned giving is one of those things that sounds way more complicated than it actually is. It's essentially a method of supporting charities that enables you to make larger gifts than you could make from ordinary income.

One popular option is a bequest in your will. This is straightforward—you just specify a gift to be made from your estate to a chosen charity in your will. It's a powerful way to ensure ongoing support for a cause you care about, even after you're gone. Plus, it can have significant tax benefits which can increase the value of your estate for your heirs while supporting good causes.

Another method is setting up a charitable trust. You transfer assets into a trust, and the trust makes donations to your chosen charities over time. You can set this up to happen during your lifetime or as part of your estate planning. This not only provides a steady stream of funding to charities but also gives you and your estate significant tax advantages.

For those who have investments, consider donating shares or securities directly to charities. This is not only tax-efficient but also allows charities to benefit from any potential growth in the value of these assets.

HACK 90- Setting Up a Philanthropic Fund

If you're looking to take your charitable efforts to the next level, setting up a philanthropic fund might be the way to go. This is like having your own charitable foundation but without the administrative hassles and high costs of setting up a separate entity.

You can do this through a community foundation which manages the fund on your behalf. You simply contribute cash, shares, or other assets into the fund when it suits you (for instance, when you sell your business or receive a bonus). The foundation then allocates grants to charities according to your interests.

One of the beauties of this setup is its flexibility. You can often recommend not only which charities are supported but also how the funds are used. Want to support educational scholarships, or fund medical research? No problem. Plus, you get to benefit from the expertise of the foundation to ensure your donations are making the most impact.

Setting up a philanthropic fund also allows you to involve your family in your charitable endeavours, fostering a tradition of giving back that can last for generations. It's a fantastic way to teach younger family members about the importance of philanthropy and the practical aspects of managing wealth for social good.

Moreover, philanthropic funds can be set up to operate during your lifetime or as a part of your legacy. This flexibility means that you can see and participate in the benefits of your giving now, adjusting your strategy as circumstances or priorities change.

In sum, when it comes to charitable considerations in crafting your legacy, it's all about making informed, strategic decisions that align with your values and goals. Whether you choose to support charities directly, engage in planned giving, or set up a philanthropic fund, each approach offers unique benefits and opportunities to ensure your wealth creates lasting positive impacts. By integrating thoughtful giving into your financial planning, you not only enrich your own life but also contribute to a richer, more vibrant community and world.

RECAP AND ACTION ITEMS ON THE

9 CRAFTING YOUR LEGACY HACKS

Crafting your legacy isn't just about securing your own future; it's about setting up a framework that benefits your loved ones and even extends to making a lasting impact in the wider world. You've now armed yourself with the tools to ensure that your estate is well-managed, your family is financially literate, and your charitable impulses are effectively channeled. Let's consolidate what you've learned and turn these insights into concrete actions.

Write Your Will:

If you haven't already, prioritize writing your will. This document is the bedrock of effective estate planning. It will ensure that your assets are distributed according to your wishes, reducing any potential conflicts after you're gone. Find a solicitor who can guide you through the legal nuances to create a watertight will.

Establish Trusts:

Consider setting up trusts to manage how your assets are used by future generations. Trusts can provide a measure of control over how your assets are distributed and when. They can also offer tax benefits, which can be a boon for preserving more of your wealth for your intended beneficiaries.

Select Your Executors:

Choosing the right executors is crucial as they will be responsible for administering your estate. Pick individuals who are not only trustworthy but also have the capability to handle financial and legal responsibilities. It might also be wise to discuss their potential role with them to ensure they are willing and prepared to take on these duties.

Educate Your Family about Finances:

Start financial education early for your children. Use everyday activities as learning experiences. This could range from setting up a savings account to involving them in budgeting household expenses. Make it interactive and fun to maintain their interest and reinforce learning.

Create a Family Budget:

If you don't already have one, establish a family budget. It's a tool that will give everyone a clear understanding of where money comes from and where it's going. Regular family meetings to discuss the budget can help in making informed decisions that align with your family's financial goals.

Involve Your Family in Financial Decisions:

Whether it's discussing major purchases or investments, involve your family in the decision-making process. This not only helps in teaching them about money management but also prepares them to make smart financial decisions in the future.

Plan Your Charitable Giving:

Decide on the causes you care about and want to support. Whether it's by setting up a philanthropic fund or engaging in planned giving, your charitable actions can form a significant part of your legacy. Research organizations that align with your values and consider how you can contribute in a way that makes a meaningful impact.

Review Regularly:

Finally, make sure to review your plans regularly. As your financial situation evolves, so too will your plans need to adapt. An annual review is a good practice to ensure that all your arrangements stay relevant and effective.

By taking these steps, you're not just planning for the future; you're actively shaping it. Remember, crafting your legacy is a dynamic process that reflects your values, vision, and the depth of your relationships. Start today, and create a legacy that feels true to who you are and the mark you wish to leave on the world.

11

CONTINUAL FINANCIAL IMPROVEMENT

"It's not how much money you make, but how much money you keep, how hard it works for you, and how many generations you keep it for." - Robert Kiyosaki

Staying Informed and Adaptive

In the ever-turbulent sea of financial waters, staying informed and adaptive isn't just a nice-to-have; it's an absolute must. Think of it as your personal GPS system in the world of finance, keeping you on course through storms and doldrums alike. This part of your journey to wealth isn't about dramatic overhauls or quick fixes. No, it's about setting a pace for continual learning, adapting, and staying ahead of the curve. Let's break this down into three fundamental practices that will keep your financial ship sailing smoothly: keeping abreast of financial news, adapting to economic changes, and embracing continuous learning.

HACK 91- Keeping Abreast of Financial News

Let's face it, the world of finance doesn't sleep, and neither does the news that drives it. But before you groan at the thought of dry, jargon-heavy financial forecasts and stock market updates, let's reshape what financial news means for you. It's not just about watching numbers fluctuate on a screen; it's about understanding how global and local events impact your wallet.

Start with finding sources that resonate with you. Whether it's financial blogs, podcasts, or magazines, choose mediums that speak in a language you understand. The Financial Times might be the gold standard for some, but if you find yourself zoning out after the first paragraph, it's not going to help. Look for commentators or financial gurus who break down complex topics into bite-sized, manageable pieces. Remember, the goal here is to stay informed, not overwhelmed.

Make it a habit. Dedicate a small chunk of your day—maybe your morning coffee time—to catch up on the latest financial news. Apps like Feedly or Flipboard can help you aggregate news from various sources into one streamlined feed, tailored to your interests. This habit isn't just about consumption; it's about gradually enhancing your financial literacy, making you more confident and competent in handling your money.

HACK 92- Adapting to Economic Changes

If there's one guarantee in the economy, it's that it will change. Prices rise and fall, markets boom and bust—all influenced by a myriad of factors that can seem dizzyingly complex. But here's a secret: you don't need a PhD in economics to effectively adapt to these changes; you just need a strategy.

Firstly, keep your financial plans flexible. Think of your budget like a living document. It should evolve as your personal circumstances and the economic environment change. For instance, if inflation is nudging up the cost of living, review and adjust your spending. Maybe swap out some non-essentials, or shop smarter to stretch your pounds further.

Secondly, always have an emergency fund, because economic downturns are when life loves to throw curveballs. This isn't just about having savings; it's about having accessible funds that can cover at least three to six months of living expenses. This buffer can be the difference between weathering a storm and being swept away by it.

Lastly, keep an eye on investment opportunities. Economic changes often open new doors. For example, a dip in the market might be a good time to buy shares at a lower price if you're in a position to do so. Remember, adapting isn't just about defense; it's about knowing when to make your move.

HACK 93- Continuous Learning

In a world where change is the only constant, learning is your best defense and a powerful tool for growth. Continuous learning in finance doesn't mean you need to bury yourself in books on economic theory—unless that's your cup of tea. It's about constantly updating your knowledge and skills relevant to your financial goals.

Start with understanding the basics of personal finance; get to grips with concepts like interest rates, inflation, investments, and taxes. These are the building blocks that will help you make informed decisions about your money. Then, move onto more advanced topics as you grow more comfortable.

Consider online courses or workshops. Platforms like Coursera and Udemy offer a range of courses taught by industry experts at little to no cost. These can be a great way to deepen your understanding of specific areas, whether it's real estate investing, stock market fundamentals, or retirement planning.

Don't overlook the value of networking. Joining groups and forums where people discuss financial strategies can expose you to new ideas and approaches. Plus, it's always helpful to have a community for support and advice.

By incorporating these three practices into your life, you're not just staying informed; you're staying ready. Ready to adapt, act, and advance regardless of what the financial forecasts throw your way. Remember, the goal of continual financial improvement isn't just about growing your wealth; it's about empowering you to lead a richer, more secure life.

Using Technology to Your Advantage

In the whirlwind world of finance, staying ahead can feel as intricate as mastering a new language. But guess what? You don't need to be a Wall Street whiz to leverage the power of technology to manage your finances like a pro. The digital age brings an array of tools at your fingertips, simplifying processes and enhancing your financial acumen. From everyday budgeting to sophisticated investment strategies, technology is your ally in building and sustaining wealth.

HACK 94- Financial Apps and Tools

Let's dive into the digital toolbox that's revolutionizing personal finance management. Imagine having a financial advisor in your pocket, constantly at your beck and call. That's essentially what financial apps are transforming into. These aren't just tools; they're your personal finance command centers.

Start with budgeting apps. Apps like Mint or YNAB (You Need A Budget) offer you a panoramic view of your finances. They link up with your bank accounts, categorize your spending, and visually represent where your money is going each month. What's more, they can help you set and stick to budgets, alerting you when you're about to overspend. It's like having a vigilant guardian angel for your wallet.

Investment apps, on the other hand, democratize the investing landscape. Consider platforms like Acorns or Nutmeg. These apps don't just facilitate investments; they make suggestions based on your financial situation and goals. With features like round-ups on purchases, they allow you to invest your spare change, literally making money while you shop.

Moreover, debt management apps like Unbury.Me provide clarity on your debts. They use the snowball or avalanche methods to show you different strategies to clear your debts faster. By seeing the numbers plainly and understanding the impact of different approaches, you can choose a strategy tailored to your financial situation.

Lastly, credit score services like Credit Karma keep you informed of your credit health, a crucial aspect of financial well-being. These services often offer insights and tips to improve your score, directly impacting your ability to secure loans with favorable terms.

Incorporating these tools into your daily financial routine doesn't just save time; it makes you more conscious of your financial status and progress. It's about making informed decisions with ease and confidence.

HACK 95- Online Investment Platforms

Gone are the days when stock markets were the playground for the elite. Now, online investment platforms have flung open the doors to the stock markets for everyone. Whether it's stocks, bonds, mutual funds, or cryptocurrencies, there's a platform that caters to your investment needs and experience level.

Platforms like E*TRADE or Robinhood simplify stock trading with user-friendly interfaces and zero commission fees on trades. These platforms not only make it easy to buy and sell stocks but also provide educational resources to boost your investing knowledge. Whether you're a novice looking to make your first investment or a seasoned trader, these platforms offer tools to help you make informed decisions.

For those inclined towards algo-trading, platforms like Interactive Brokers offer advanced tools that allow you to automate your trading strategies. This means you can set up algorithms to buy or sell securities based on specific market conditions, enabling you to make money while you sleep.

Furthermore, if you're interested in a more hands-off approach, robo-advisors such as Wealthfront and Betterment can manage your investments for you. By using algorithms to assess risk tolerance and financial goals, they automatically adjust your portfolio to align with your long-term financial aspirations. It's a set-it-and-forget-it approach that ensures your investments are continually optimized without daily oversight.

HACK 96- Security Measures for Digital Finance

With great power comes great responsibility, particularly when it involves your financial data. Cybersecurity is non-negotiable in the digital finance world. Here's how you can fortify your financial fortress against potential digital threats.

Firstly, embrace strong, unique passwords for each financial account. Tools like LastPass or 1Password can manage your passwords, ensuring they are robust and secure without the hassle of remembering each one.

Secondly, two-factor authentication (2FA) is your next line of defense. Most financial platforms offer 2FA, where you would need to verify your identity using two different methods before accessing your account. This could be a combination of something you know (password), something you have (a mobile device), or something you are (fingerprint or facial recognition).

Moreover, be vigilant about phishing attacks. Always verify the authenticity of emails requesting financial information. Phishers often mimic reputable companies to steal sensitive data. If an email asks for such information, contact the company directly using a trusted number or email.

Lastly, keep your software updated. This includes your mobile devices, computers, and any applications you use for financial management. Updates often include security patches that protect against new threats.

Reflecting and Revising Regularly

HACK 97- Annual financial check-ups

Think of your financial health like your physical health. Just as you'd visit the doctor each year for your annual check-up, your finances deserve the same attention and care through regular reviews. This isn't just about checking how much you've saved or if you've hit your targets—it's a holistic look at your entire financial landscape.

Start by pulling together all your financial statements—bank accounts, investments, loans, credit cards, and any other financial obligations or assets. It's like laying all the pieces of a puzzle on the table before you start connecting them. Seeing everything in one place can provide a clearer picture of where you stand and what needs your attention.

Next, analyze your income versus your spending over the past year. Have your earnings increased? Fantastic! But have your expenditures crept up too? Often, as people earn more, they start spending more, sometimes without even noticing—this is called lifestyle creep. It's natural to want to indulge or upgrade your lifestyle when you have more disposable income, but unchecked, it can hamper your long-term financial goals.

Look at your savings and investments. Are they growing according to your expectations and targets? If not, why? This could be due to a variety of reasons, such as market downturns, insufficient contributions, or high fees. Understanding these factors can help you decide whether to stick with your current strategies or explore new options.

Consider also any debts you have. Check if you're managing them well or if there are opportunities to refinance or consolidate to reduce interest rates and monthly payments. Sometimes, shifting a credit card balance to a lower-interest option or restructuring your mortgage can save you significant amounts in the long run.

Lastly, review your financial protection measures, such as insurance (life, health, property). Are they adequate? As life changes, your coverage might need to be adjusted to ensure it still meets your needs and those of your dependents.

HACK 98- Revising financial goals

Your financial goals aren't set in stone. They shift as your life unfolds—new career opportunities, changes in family dynamics, or even evolving personal priorities can all influence what you aim for financially. That's why revising your goals is not just necessary; it's a crucial part of staying on track towards a richer, more secure life.

Start by reflecting on the goals you set last year. Which ones did you achieve? Celebrate these wins—small or big, they're all steps in the right direction. For the goals you haven't hit, think about why. Was it a lack of resources? Did unexpected expenses throw you off course? Or perhaps the goals were too ambitious? Understanding these can help you set more realistic or different targets this time around.

Now, think about the coming year. What do you want to achieve? Perhaps you're aiming to save a certain amount, invest in learning a new skill, or maybe you're planning a major life event like buying a home or starting a family. Ensure your goals are SMART: Specific, Measurable, Achievable, Relevant, and Time-bound. This framework doesn't just add structure—it makes your goals more tangible and attainable.

Adjust your financial plan to align with these revised goals. This might involve shifting your budget, altering your savings strategy, or even changing your investment approach. Remember, the plan is your roadmap; keep it updated and relevant to the terrain you're navigating.

HACK 99- Seeking feedback and advice

No man is an island, and this holds particularly true when it comes to financial planning. Seeking external feedback and advice can provide fresh perspectives, uncover overlooked opportunities, or highlight potential pitfalls in your strategies.

Start with your inner circle. Family and friends might provide insights into your spending habits or investment choices, often from a place of personal understanding and shared experiences. However, remember they might not always have the expertise needed to give comprehensive financial advice.

This is where financial advisors come in. A good advisor can offer professional, unbiased guidance tailored to your specific circumstances. They can help you navigate complex financial landscapes, from investments and savings to taxes and retirement planning. When choosing an advisor, look for credentials, testimonials from clients, and ensure they understand your goals and risk tolerance.

Additionally, consider joining financial workshops or seminars. These can be valuable resources for learning and networking. They not only enhance your knowledge but also connect you with like-minded individuals who can share their experiences and advice.

Lastly, don't underestimate the power of books, podcasts, and reputable financial news sources. These can provide ongoing education and keep you informed about economic trends and new financial tools. Just remember to critically evaluate the information and consider how it applies to your personal situation.

In conclusion, reflecting on and revising your financial strategies regularly is essential. It's not just about keeping on top of your finances; it's about actively shaping them to serve you better, ensuring that each year brings you closer to a richer and more fulfilling life.

RECAP AND ACTION ITEMS ON THE 9 CONTINUAL FINANCIAL IMPROVEMENT HACKS

So, you've navigated through the essentials of staying informed and adaptive, harnessing technology to bolster your financial prowess, and the importance of regular reflection and revision. Now, it's time to roll up your sleeves and put these insights into action. Remember, the goal here is to not just read about improvement but to make it a tangible part of your financial journey.

Set up your financial news feed:

Choose two or three reliable financial news sources and subscribe to their updates. Tools like Feedly or Flipboard can help you consolidate news feeds in one place. This will help you keep abreast of important economic events without feeling overwhelmed.

Embrace technology:

If you haven't already, download a comprehensive financial app that allows you to track your spending, investments, and savings all in one place. Apps like Mint or YNAB (You Need A Budget) are great places to start. Spend some time each week exploring features within these apps that you haven't used—there might be budgeting tools or investment tracking options that could give you a clearer picture of your financial health.

Tighten your digital security:

Update your passwords and consider using a password manager. Enable two-factor authentication on all financial accounts to add an extra layer of security.

Schedule your annual financial review:

Set a recurring date in your calendar, perhaps the start of a new financial year, to review your financial status. Assess what's working and what's not. This is a great time to adjust your budgets, rethink your investment strategies, and set new financial targets.

Keep your goals flexible:

As you refine your financial strategies, allow your goals to evolve based on your current economic reality and personal aspirations. Sometimes, shifting a goal post is not a sign of setback but of smarter strategy.

Seek professional advice:

Even if you're confident in your financial acumen, a fresh perspective from a financial advisor can offer new insights and help you avoid blind spots.

Engage in continuous learning:

Dedicate at least an hour a week to learning more about personal finance and investment strategies. Whether through books, podcasts, or online courses, expanding your knowledge will empower you to make more informed decisions.

By taking these steps, you will not only strengthen your financial foundation but also enhance your ability to adapt to whatever economic changes may come your way. Wealth isn't just about having money; it's about having options and the freedom to make choices that enrich your life. Stay curious, stay informed, and most importantly, stay proactive in managing your money.

EMBARKING ON YOUR FINANCIAL FREEDOM JOURNEY

As you turn the pages of this guide, you have journeyed through a meticulously curated roadmap towards financial liberation. The strategies and insights shared are designed not only to inform but also to transform. The goal has always been to equip you with the tools necessary to navigate the complex terrain of personal finance with confidence and agility.

The mastery of money management is akin to learning a new language or instrument; it requires patience, practice, and perseverance. You have been introduced to various techniques—from unveiling the mysteries of money, ditching debt, to creatively cutting costs and augmenting your income. Each chapter built upon the last, creating a comprehensive framework to support your financial well-being.

However, the journey does not conclude here. The true essence of this knowledge lies in its application. It's about making those small, consistent changes that compound over time, leading to monumental shifts in your financial status and, more importantly, your life.

Imagine a future where financial worries are not a constant

source of stress, where you are not living paycheck to paycheck, but instead, enjoying the freedom to make choices that align with your deepest desires and values. This is not just a distant dream but a tangible reality that you can achieve with the tools and insights you now possess.

The path to financial independence is uniquely yours. The strategies discussed can and should be adapted to fit your individual circumstances and goals. Whether it is through smarter spending on social media, innovative cost-cutting, or exploring new avenues for income, the key is to take action. Start small if you must, but start today. Every step you take is a step closer to financial autonomy.

As you implement these strategies, remember that the landscape of personal finance is ever-evolving. Staying informed and adaptable is crucial. Challenges will arise, but equipped with the right knowledge and a resilient mindset, you will be able to navigate through them.

Moreover, the journey towards financial freedom is not one to be walked alone. Engaging with a community of like-minded individuals, seeking professional advice when needed, and sharing your own experiences can enhance your journey. Learning from others and contributing your insights can provide not only support but also inspiration.

Remember, the decision to seek help is a testament to your commitment to your financial health and should be viewed as a proactive step towards achieving your goals. It is an investment in your future, one that can yield substantial returns in terms of peace of mind and financial security.

You have the tools, you have the knowledge, and now, it's about taking those bold steps towards realizing your potential. It's about not just dreaming of a better financial future but actively constructing it with each decision you make. It's about not just surviving financially but thriving, creating a life where your financial decisions support your life goals and aspirations.

Let this book serve as a cornerstone of your financial journey, a guide that you can return to time and again. As you grow and evolve, so too will your financial strategies. Keep learning, keep experimenting, and most importantly, keep pushing forward. The road to financial freedom is perpetual and persistent pursuit.

Your financial freedom journey is just beginning, and the possibilities are limitless. Embrace the challenge with enthusiasm and optimism. Forge ahead with the confidence that you are well-equipped to not only meet but exceed your financial goals.

In closing, take a moment to reflect on all that you have learnt. Allow yourself to feel empowered by the knowledge you have gained. Then, step forward into your future, a future where you are in control of your finances and, by extension, your life.

Your journey to financial independence is yours to shape. Make it a remarkable one.

Enjoyed the book?

If this book helped you or brought you some enjoyment, please take a moment to leave a quick review online.

It only takes a minute, but it makes a huge difference to me and helps others discover the book too.

Your feedback means the world and thanks for your support!

www.ingramcontent.com/pod-product-compliance
Lightning Source LLC
Chambersburg PA
CBHW071922210526
45479CB00002B/513